ICE STORM

Written by
Molly Taylor Sanchez

Cover illustration by Anna Speshilova

Cover design by Phillip Colhouer

goodandbeautiful.com

TABLE OF CONTENTS

CHAPTER 1

CANADIAN WINTER

"Aha! It's working!" Esme Errard exclaimed as the radio she was tinkering with crackled to life. It was an old one she had been trying to wire up to a six-volt battery, changing it from a wall-plug radio to a battery-operated radio. Working with electronics was a bit of an unusual hobby for an eleven-year-old girl on a dairy farm, but ever since she had done a short homeschool unit on electricity a couple of years ago, she'd been captivated by the subject.

Esme scooped up the old machine with the battery duct-taped to its side, wires springing in every direction, and ran the short distance from her back door to the barn, her mid-length blonde hair trailing behind her. Esme's sky-blue eyes, broad forehead, and ear-to-ear smile contrasted significantly with the rest of her family. Her mother always said she took after her grandmother, who also shared her spunk and determination.

Lilou, her maman; Jérôme, her papa; and her sixteen-year-old brother, Luc, all had brown eyes. Maman and Luc shared Esme's blonde hair, while her papa's was brown, and it was rare to see him without a short scruff on his face. Luc was shorter than Papa, but broad shouldered and muscular, another disparity with Esme's extra-small frame.

As Esme entered the barn, her family members each held a hand towel, wiping down the milking parlor, the cows already having been led to their stalls. Esme turned up the radio's volume, beaming with pride. Lilou, Jérôme, and Luc tossed their towels into a bucket and gathered around.

"*Tu l'as fait!*" her father exclaimed. "I'm not sure I'd be able to do that. You're going to have to show me how it works when we go in the house."

"Nice job, Sis," Luc said. "That's pretty cool."

The family all eagerly turned toward the radio as the weather report began. "I hope you are enjoying your Sunday evening before another work week begins. Be sure to take your umbrella and get out the ice melt tomorrow! Weather reports call for freezing rain beginning as early as tomorrow morning and lasting through Tuesday from eastern Ontario into all of southern Quebec. Parts of New Brunswick could also be affected. If you're new to the area, you may not know what an ice storm is. The phenomenon happens when warm air comes up from the south and sits right on top of a thin layer of Arctic air from the north, which is at ground level. The rain falls through the warm air and has no time to become snow before it hits the ground, where it freezes on contact and forms a blanket of sparkling ice. This one looks like it could be a doozy, so remember to use caution while driving, and don't be in a hurry on the roads."

"Did you know that was coming?" Lilou asked, turning to Jérôme as she closed a gate to the milking parlor.

"You mean the ice storm?" Jérôme asked. "They mentioned it on the weather report last night. Not to worry. We have the generator and pole switch if we have an outage," he added as he climbed back into the tractor attached to the feed wagon. The pole switch was simply an outdoor box to which a generator could be plugged in, and electricity could still run to the house and barn without the need for rewiring.

"Do you want to learn how to hook up the box scraper and clean the walkways?" Lilou asked Esme, opening the gate to the skid steer loader. Lilou was small like Esme, but she could drive a tractor as well as anyone.

"Um, I'd better take this radio back in the house," Esme said. She hurried past the heifers happily chewing their silage, across the yard, and back into the house. Esme was not like Luc; learning to run farm equipment was the last thing she wanted to do. Because of her size, the tractors, equipment, and even the cows seemed enormous and intimidating. None of it felt safe to her. She liked electricity because of its laws and adherence to the rules of physics, which Esme found comforting—and mostly predictable. Besides, she hated getting dirty.

She set down her radio on the kitchen table, and the pile of unwashed dinner dishes caught her eye. Turning on the hot water, she sighed as the warmth hit her hands, which were chilled from her quick jaunt outside. She picked up the nearest pot and began rhythmically scrubbing the oatmeal bits crusted onto the bottom. If she wasn't going to help with the farm chores, she figured she ought to contribute somehow.

Just as she was putting the last plate in the dishwasher, her walkie-talkie sounded with Morse code beeps. "Meet in the tunnel," they spelled out.

Esme haphazardly dried her hands and then lunged for her walkie-talkie. She replied with a series of short and long tones spelling out "okay." Grabbing her coat and a flashlight, Esme wrote a hasty note to her family on the whiteboard magnetized to the fridge: *In the tunnel. —E.* She bounded out the door to the root cellar behind their home.

She heaved the door from the ground, scrambled down the steps, and reached for the pull chain to switch on the light. The cellar was lined in old multicolored bricks and stones set with mortar. Stepping around large bins stocked with potatoes, onions, and carrots, Esme wound her way to the back wall of the cellar. Most people would not notice the narrow gap in the corner of the back wall. Esme slipped around the corner and through the opening into a brick-lined tunnel.

The tunnel ended in the maple forest some twenty yards behind the home of Alice Giroux, Esme's best friend. On the Giroux end of the tunnel, steps went straight up to a door that opened directly into the forest. The maple farm—or sugar bush, as everyone called it—was located in southwestern Quebec and had been in the Giroux family for four generations. The Errard family had moved to the dairy farm only three years ago, when Esme was eight and Alice nine. Alice had discovered that a church used to stand where the Errard home was built; the tunnel, however, had always been a bit of a mystery, its purpose lost with those who built it. Esme wondered what stories these bricks held.

The two families kept the tunnel swept and clean, free of cobwebs, dirt, and leaves. Esme and Alice spent hours in the cool, damp underground passageway playing out all kinds of make-believe scenarios, from princesses escaping an evil king to refugees hiding during a war. They pretended it was their underground bunker during a nuclear attack, with plenty of snacks and soft, warm blankets, of course. About the length of a football field, it was the perfect place to meet up in the winter because, protected from the elements, it was always slightly warmer than the temperature above.

In the summer the two friends spent a great deal of time in the maple forest. A year and a half before, the girls had helped Alice's father build a treehouse in the boughs of a three-hundred-year-old maple. Complete with a metal staircase, a roof, and large glass windows, it also had a balcony with a railing made from twisted, gnarly branches. Hanging from the floor of the treehouse was a rope swing with a wide wooden slat that the two girls could sit on together, and next to it was a simple wooden picnic table with attached benches. It was also a make-believe paradise. Esme especially loved the treehouse in the fall, when the trees' leaves turned gold, burnt orange, and crimson with flecks of green that were reminiscent of summer days.

The Giroux sugar shack stood on the forest's edge, near their drive. It had started as a shed for boiling and processing the syrup, but Alice's family had expanded it by building tables and benches inside and out, and it had become quite an attraction in early spring. Tourists from all over Canada and beyond would come for hearty soups and stews and, of course, all things maple, including pancakes, maple sugar pie, donuts with maple glaze, and the most popular: maple taffy. Each person could create their own taffy by pouring a line of syrup on a pile of snow, letting the sweet drizzle cool for a few minutes, and then rolling a popsicle stick across the line to make a taffy lollipop.

Esme and Alice loved helping (and indulging) at the

sugar shack. The Girouxs paid the girls to wipe down tables and help serve food. It was an opportunity for the French-speaking pair to practice English with English-speaking patrons. They had also been introduced to German, Spanish, Italian, and even Arabic.

The tunnel, tree house, and sugar shack were Esme's escape from the dairy farm. Besides shying away from the cattle and equipment, she was lactose intolerant, so she couldn't even enjoy what her family spent their waking hours producing.

Esme and Alice kept their walkie-talkies on all the time when they were apart, except at night and during homeschool hours from nine to noon. They almost always communicated over the walkie-talkies in Morse code, something the girls both learned because it felt more mysterious and exciting; they could send messages no one around them would understand.

"Alice!" Esme exclaimed as she caught the glimmer of another flashlight coming toward her in the rustic tunnel.

Alice and Esme were so excited that they nearly collided as they ran toward each other, their flashlights bouncing beams of light through the corridor.

"I have big news!" Alice exclaimed breathlessly.

CHAPTER 2

WARNINGS IN THE WIND

"What is it?" Esme asked, her curiosity piqued. "It must be good for a summoning to the tunnel."

"I was talking to Maman about things I could do to make money for that bicycle I've been wanting from Joe's Sports Shop, and we came up with the most amazing idea—and I want you to help me do it!"

"Make some money? What? Tell me!" Esme pressed, her excitement sparked by Alice's. "Something better than wiping down tables in the sugar shack?"

"*Way* better than wiping tables in the sugar shack!" Alice assured, her playful green eyes wide with mystery, the freckles across her nose and cheeks scrunching into a cheerful smile. She seemed to relish holding Esme in suspense.

Reaching up—because Alice was a few inches taller—Esme grabbed her friend by the shoulders. "Tell me!" Alice's chin-length brown hair wobbled with Esme's shaking.

Alice giggled. "Okay! We are going to have . . ." she paused for dramatic effect.

"Yeah?" Esme playfully shook Alice's shoulders again.

". . . a forest adventure camp for kids!" she exclaimed, clapping her hands together. "We can plan lots of activities. Maman said parents would be happy to pay for their kids to have a fun, educational experience. And she said she can help. But you and I can plan all the activities!"

"Esme!" a voice called through the tunnel. It sounded like Luc. "We need you to come help us do some prep work for the animals before the storm hits."

"Okay!" Esme called back. "Be right there!"

"Don't be long." Luc knew her well.

"So? Do you want to do the adventure camp with me?" Alice asked.

"Is the ocean wet?" Esme joked. "Of course I do! I'm in! When do we start?"

"That's one of the details we'll have to talk about and plan," Alice said. "But you'd better go. Meet me tomorrow?"

"Yes! At noon?" asked Esme.

"Sounds good! See you then! I'll bring peanut butter and maple sandwiches!"

"I'll bring apple slices!"

"Bye!" The friends hugged, each buoyant with excitement and anticipation about their new idea.

By the time Esme emerged from the root cellar, dusk had turned to darkness. There was a noticeable uptick in wind speed and a drop in temperature as a gust whipped across her face, disheveling her blonde hair and biting at her cheeks and neck. She ran quickly to the barn, where Jérôme, Luc, and Lilou were busy at work.

"I made sure all the troughs are completely full, in both the milk barn and the heifer barn, as well as the yards outside," Luc reported.

"Okay, come help me move the generator close to the pole switch," Jérôme said to Luc. "Esme, do you think you can manage to bring the gas can over? It's full." Papa pointed to the corner of the barn where a red five-gallon jerry can stood. "You can scoot it onto the skid steer and drive it over to make it easy."

Drive the can over on the skid steer? Did Papa not realize she didn't know how to drive it? At that moment she was wishing she had allowed her mother to show her how to operate the small tractor earlier. She walked over to the jerry can, wrapped her fingers around the handle, and heaved it up. *Maybe I can just carry it over*, she thought. But she only made it about a foot, shuffling with all her might, before she had to set it down. The can was impossibly heavy. Esme wanted to be helpful. She eyed the tractor, which was parked about ten yards from the jerry can, with trepidation. Should she try to drive it?

Lilou must have noticed Esme's dilemma. She hurried over, hopped in the skid steer, drove it to the jerry can, and lifted the can carefully onto the bucket. Then she drove the tractor outside to where Jérôme and Luc had moved the generator.

Esme trotted behind Lilou and the small tractor. She was curious about the generator and wanted to see how it worked.

Her papa saw her and said, "Esme, can you grab my heavy-duty extension cord and bring it over? It's the yellow one."

Glad to have something she could do easily, Esme ran back through the open barn door. The extension cords dangled from hooks on the wall, about six different coils in varied lengths and colors—too high for her to reach. Esme looked around for something she could stand on. Grabbing a black feed bucket, she turned it over and stepped up on it. Stretching her arm as far as she could, she just managed to wrap her fingertips around the yellow extension cord Jérôme had looped into a neat bundle. Lifting up on her tiptoes, she attempted to sling the stack of coils up over the utility hook. Suddenly, the bucket shifted under her, and Esme strained to control her wavering legs, torso, and arms. Attempting to adjust her footing, she stepped on the bucket's edge, making it flip and crash to its side, bringing Esme down with a *smack* on the concrete floor.

Her shoulder and hip throbbed with pain. What was worse, her whole family had witnessed the entire mishap. They all rushed over.

"Esme!" Lilou shouted.

"Are you okay?" Luc asked.

"Just sit tight; don't move," Jérôme said, kneeling next to her.

A powerful gale blew so hard it rattled the barn walls. Several of the cows bellowed in response.

Esme noticed then that her head hurt as well. She reached for her temple and grimaced at the pain.

"Don't touch it," her maman cautioned. "Luc, go grab a towel, please."

Esme was startled when she saw blood on her fingers. *Don't cry; be tough*, she thought. Still humiliated from the fall, she didn't want to compound her embarrassment by crying. *I wish I was more help around the farm*, she thought dejectedly, yearning to be useful like her brother. Her mental anguish stung more than the physical pain.

Jérôme was looking closely into her eyes when Luc ran back with a dry towel as well as a wet one.

"Her pupils don't appear dilated," her father noted. "Hopefully she doesn't have a concussion. Do you think you can sit up?" he then asked, gently helping her.

"I'm fine," Esme said, sitting up easily as Lilou wiped her temple.

"Here, hold that there," Lilou instructed, pressing the folded dry towel to Esme's head.

"I want to see you stand on your own before I carry you into the house," Jérôme said.

Esme stood. "I'm fine, Papa. I can walk. Thank you," she told him, holding the towel to her head. *Not only am I incapable of helping, now I am taking everyone away from their work*, Esme sulked as she walked back to the house, Lilou next to her.

"Here, sit down," Lilou said, pulling out a kitchen chair for her daughter and then reaching for a box of supplies in the pantry. "Let me clean that up and bandage it for you," her mother said gently, taking the towel from Esme's hand and closely examining the wound on her temple.

"I'm sorry," Esme whimpered.

"You're sorry? What on earth for?" Maman wet a clean washcloth in warm water and then carefully dabbed the cut.

"For being so useless on the farm," Esme said, tears pooling in her eyes.

"Nonsense!" Lilou said as she pulled out a box full of bandages in all shapes and sizes.

"I can't do anything right! Luc is more capable and helpful on the farm than I will ever be."

"Now you listen to me," her mother said firmly, putting the box down and looking Esme straight in the eyes. "Your worth is not determined by what you can do or by how strong you are. You hear me? We love you for who you are, not for what you can do. We love you because you are ours. What you do is just part of who you are. Do you know what I mean?"

"So what I do doesn't even matter?" Esme questioned through her tears.

"It only matters because it makes you more you."

"What does that mean?" Esme asked, trying to process her mother's words through the throbbing pain in her head.

"What we do each day, each moment, draws us closer to God or moves us away. When our actions glorify God, He makes us more of who we can become. Our joy grows as we move closer to Him. But His love is infinite and unchanging simply because we are His, not because of anything we do. Does that make sense?"

"Um, I guess."

"Think of it this way: Little babies completely depend on our care. Do we think less of them because they can't do anything productive? Sleeping, eating, growing, creating messes, making mistakes, falling down over and over—those are all part of their growth. But do we love them more when they can finally walk? Or say a word? Of course not. We love them because we have sacrificed so much for their well-being, and they are ours. What I am saying is, never measure how precious you are to God or to this family based on what you are able to do or not do. You are infinitely precious because you are ours. Period."

"Okay. I think I get it. Thank you, Maman."

"You're welcome," she said as she gave Esme a tight squeeze. "Now, let's get this wound fixed up, shall we?" She smoothed on some antibiotic ointment, pinched the cut together to add a couple of butterfly bandages, and then covered the whole area with a large adhesive bandage.

About that time, Jérôme and Luc walked in the door, bringing a *whoosh* of cold air with them.

"Wow! It's wild out there tonight!" Jérôme exclaimed as the door slammed behind him.

CHAPTER 3

ICE DESCENDS

Monday morning, the Errard family's day began at four thirty as usual. Esme's father had told her the night before that she didn't need to help with chores in the morning—to go ahead and sleep in to let her body heal after her fall. However, Esme's internal clock popped her eyes open like a jack-in-the-box right at a quarter to five. Her shoulder and hip ached when she rolled over to go back to sleep, reminding her of last night's mishap.

The rain has already started, she thought. She could hear the tinkling on her window and the steady *tap-tap-tap* on the roof. A flush of the toilet, the swinging of the bathroom door, a shuffling down the hallway, and the creaking stairs announced that Luc was on his way to start the milking. Her papa would already be out filling the feed loader with a mixture of grain and silage for the milk cows.

Esme heard the murmuring of morning greetings between Luc and their maman, followed by the bang of the back door, and then silence, except for the dance of heavy raindrops that sounded all around her.

Suddenly, Esme's memory of her meeting in the tunnel with Alice lit upon her mind like a butterfly on a daisy—delight rushed through her body. *A forest adventure camp for kids! Oh yeah! I can't wait to meet Alice in the tunnel to make plans!* Esme's heart began thumping with eager anticipation, and she could not lie in bed any longer. She hopped up and dressed warmly in a wool sweater and jeans, deciding she felt well enough to help in the barn. The sooner the morning chores were done, the sooner homeschool would be completed, and she would be free to design the adventure camp with her best friend.

Even her pain subsided as happy thoughts of the project buoyed brightly in her mind. Neither an ice storm, nor bruises, nor farm chores could bring her down. At the back door, she slipped on her boots and coat, pulled a warm wool *tuque* onto her head—being extra careful of the bandage—and hurried out the door. Ice crunched under her feet, and she paused for a moment, remembering that she should slow down and walk carefully to avoid another tumble. Still, she was glad to feel the stiffness in her shoulder and hip melting away with the movement. Thankfully, they didn't seem to have been injured too badly by her fall the day before.

While Luc milked the herd in the parlor end of the barn, it was Esme's job to rake the empty stalls, scraping the manure and soiled sawdust into the barn gutters, which would be swept out by the motorized barn cleaner. Henri and Pierre, the farmhands Jérôme had hired to help, were already working in the stalls when Esme walked in.

The loud rumble of the rain on the barn roof added to the whirring of the ventilation fans.

"Why, Miss Esme," Henri shouted over the noise, "we didn't think you would be joining us this morning." He flashed his bright white smile, a deep contrast to his dark skin. Pierre waved a gloved hello from the other end of the barn. Pierre was wiry compared to Henri's muscular stockiness, and he was younger than Henri, but he could move just as fast as his counterpart when clearing the muck from the stalls.

Esme flushed, wondering if Henri and Pierre knew about her tumble and the distraction her clumsiness had caused the previous evening.

"Morning, Henri," Esme said. She waved at Pierre. While she couldn't literally dig into the work due to her bruised shoulder, Esme appreciated feeling useful as she trotted back and forth between the two men, helping with lighter tasks and bringing them tools and equipment as needed.

They were about halfway through cleaning the stalls when the lights in the barn shut off, as well as the fans, leaving them in complete darkness. It was only six o'clock in the morning on January 5, so dawn wouldn't break for a couple more hours. The pounding of the rain on the roof suddenly went from mildly threatening to downright hostile.

It was just a few moments before Esme saw a beam of light, and then another, as Henri walked toward her with two flashlights and handed her one. Pierre joined them.

"You go check on Luc in the milking parlor," Henri shouted to Esme over the roar of the rain. Turning to Pierre, he continued, "Let's go out and get the generator running."

Esme hurried through the barn and around the corner to the milking parlor. Luc already had a flashlight of his own. The cows were agitated, bellowing at the sudden darkness during milking. Some were stamping their feet in their stalls.

"You stay here with the cows!" Luc said. "I'll go get the generator running!" He took off before Esme had a chance to tell him that Henri and Pierre were already on it.

In less than a minute, the lights were back on. Jérôme, Lilou, Luc, Henri, and Pierre all converged in the milking parlor.

"We have electricity," said Jérôme, "but the power is not what we're used to. It's not enough to run everything at once. We need to keep the well water pump and the ventilation fans going as long as possible. On top of that, the generator can only handle two other motors at a time. So for now, we will run the milker pump and the cooler tank. The well pump, the silo unloaders, and the gutter cleaners will have to stay off."

"Is there power to the house?" Lilou asked.

"Yes, lights and heat should be on as long as the generator is running," Jérôme said. "Hopefully the grid will be back up before long."

Lilou turned to Esme. "I haven't yet had a chance to wish you good morning! How are you feeling? No headache or anything this morning?"

Esme shook her head. "Just a little bruised on my shoulder and hip. Otherwise, I feel great!"

Lilou carefully peeled back her daughter's *tuque*, checking on the bandages. "It looks like this is healing well! I think you'll be okay to resume your regular chores and activities as long as you feel like you can. I'm so grateful you weren't hurt worse!" She pulled her daughter into a warm hug, and Esme relished her mother's concern and affection. Lilou gave Esme a final squeeze and then looked around. "The men seem to have things under control out here. Let's go make some breakfast, shall we?"

The walk back to the house was almost comical. The rain was still pounding down, but it instantly froze on contact with any exposed surface, creating a sheet of ice across the ground. Esme and Lilou slipped and slid the whole way across the yard.

“We’d better strap on our ice cleats next time we go out!” Lilou said, the two of them giggling as they shuffled awkwardly in the darkness, holding onto one another.

They made a tall stack of pancakes, plus eggs and sausage, served along with a pitcher of orange juice and a small glass jug of maple syrup gifted by the Giroux family at Christmas.

Lilou turned the oven on to warm and placed the pancakes, eggs, and sausage inside. “Why don’t you go ahead and eat while it’s hot, Esme? I’ll see what else needs to be done out there.”

“Don’t forget your ice cleats,” Esme said as she opened the oven and piled some food on a white plate. She drizzled the syrup over her entire breakfast, then kissed the jug and smiled at the *Giroux Maple Farms* sticker on it. Her tummy still fluttered with excitement about the adventure camp—or maybe it was growling in anticipation of a delicious meal. Either way, Esme planned to start working on her schoolwork immediately so that she would be ready to meet Alice at noon for their first planning session.

Halfway through her lesson on Canadian history, Esme looked up as Lilou, Jérôme, Luc, Henri, and Pierre trudged in from the relentless storm. “Ah, it smells so good in here,” exhaled Jérôme.

Esme smiled. She looked at the clock. It was just before nine. They usually finished with chores around seven.

"Esme, you have got to come see this," Luc said, a huge smile on his face.

Certain that her growing teenage brother would be famished after an extended morning of chores, Esme was surprised that whatever he wanted to show her held more notable value than food. What could it possibly be? A baby raccoon? Or perhaps a two-headed calf? She could hardly imagine what Luc would care about more than eating.

Getting out of her chair, she gingerly stretched her leg and then followed Luc to the back door as everyone else began filling their plates with food. She pulled on her boots and coat, tucked her hood over her head, and followed her big brother out the back door.

"Ahh!" Esme gasped. "It's beautiful!"

Luc grinned, watching her reaction to the sudden change in scenery. It was still raining, but the clouds had parted in the east, and the morning sun was peeking through the storm. Everything in sight had donned a crystalline sheath.

There was a peaceful stillness, almost a reverence, as nature humbly accepted the robe of ornate beauty that had been placed upon her. The trees actually appeared to bow. Esme reached out her hands, palms up, and turned in circles, taking it all in, feeling the icy rain on her face. She said a silent prayer of gratitude for this gift of beauty.

"We need to take some pictures!" she said to Luc.

"You go ahead; I'm gonna eat!"

"Thank you for showing me this, Luc. I don't know how I missed it earlier!" she exclaimed.

"It was too dark," Luc reminded her. "Plus, the longer it rains, the more icy everything becomes. Those icicles are growing by the minute!" he said, pointing to the pattern of icy spears running across the length of their roof.

Just then, the clouds converged, shrouding the sun. Esme no longer felt an urgency to go grab a camera but was simply appreciating the present moment. "It just kind of feels like a love note, doesn't it?"

"A love note? What do you mean?" asked Luc.

"Surrounded by such beauty with the sun shining through for just a few moments—don't you think it was like a little love note from Heaven? Like God gave you and me that moment—created all of it—just to show us that He loves us."

Suddenly, a rumble of thunder rolled across the heavens.

Luc smiled. "You just might be right," he said.

CHAPTER 4

DO UNTO OTHERS

The phone calls began at eleven o'clock on Monday morning as Esme was finishing up her schoolwork for the day. Their landline had two receivers in the house as well as one in each of the two barns.

"Hello? Errard residence," Esme answered. Then she heard her father pick up the phone in the barn.

"Hello. Jérôme Errard," he answered, not realizing Esme had answered the call a moment before him.

"Jérôme, bless you for answering." Esme didn't mean to eavesdrop, but the desperation in the caller's voice captivated her attention. "We didn't get to the milking this morning before the power shut off. We didn't think it would be off this long, and now the cows are bawling because their udders are so full. And there's no way we can milk fifty cows by hand, you know. The cows won't tolerate it, even if our hands could take it," said the voice.

"Of course you can't milk them by hand," Jérôme said knowingly. "Listen, come get our generator."

"Oh, bless you, bless you," the man said.

"Do you have a pole switch?"

"No, we only have the panel boxes."

"Okay, you will need to have an electrician come and hook it up and then change it from box to box if you need it in more than one place," Jérôme said.

"Of course, of course. I will call Germaine right now. He can do that, and I will be there in ten minutes to get the generator if that's okay with you."

"Come on over, Brewster," said Jérôme. "Be careful on the roads."

"Thank you a million times, Jérôme."

As the call ended, it dawned on Esme that lending the generator to the neighbor meant no more power at home until the generator was returned.

The phone rang again immediately after they hung up. Esme didn't pick up this time, knowing her papa could get it. She turned to Luc, who was at the computer writing an essay.

"Luc! Papa is lending out the generator to another farmer!"

"What? Did you just listen in on the whole conversation?" he asked.

Esme blushed. "I guess I did. I didn't mean to. But did you hear what I said? Someone is coming to get the generator in ten minutes, which means . . ."

Understanding dawned on Luc. "Which means we won't have lights. Or heat. Or a microwave or music or hot water . . ." A concerned look spread across his face.

"Maman had better hurry with her shower," Esme said, knowing her mother had just barely had a chance to go clean up after the disarray of the morning routine.

A minute later, the phone rang again. Just once. Jérôme must have picked up the call in the barn.

Moments after, Jérôme burst into the house, breathless, with icy droplets atop his fur felt cowboy hat. "If anyone calls looking for a generator, tell them we have already lent ours out to two other dairy farmers. Tell them we are sorry, but there simply isn't enough time for anyone else to use it. If I'm correct in my calculations, once these two are finished, it will be time for our evening milking, and that's pushing it. I've already had to turn someone down."

Lilou hurried down the stairs, wrapped up in her long teal robe, hair wet, rubbing moisturizer on her face and neck. "What's going on?" she asked.

"Luc and Esme can fill you in, sweetie. I need to get back out to help Henri and Pierre load up the generator for Brewster."

Lilou's confused expression turned to her two children as Jérôme hurried back outside into the pouring rain.

"Papa has lent out the generator to a couple of other farmers to do their milking," Esme said as the phone rang again. "One of them is coming to pick it up now."

Luc picked up the phone. "Hello, Errard residence." Esme and Lilou watched him intently as he listened to the caller on the other end. "We have one, but I'm sorry to tell you that our father has already lent it to two other farms to do their milking . . . okay . . . I'm very sorry. I hope it works out for you . . . bye."

As Luc hung up, the lights in the house blinked off. The hum of the refrigerator hushed, as well as the fan for the central heating. The computer screen went dark. The only sound then was the rhythmic drum of rainfall outside.

"Aw, my essay! I didn't have a chance to save it! Why don't people just get their own generators?" Luc growled.

Esme picked up the phone and put it to her ear, listening for the low buzz of a dial tone. "At least we still have the phone line," she said.

"I spent an hour working on that, and I'll have to start all over!" Luc complained bitterly.

"It's not usually very convenient to help those in need," said their mother gently, "but it is the right thing to do. You can rewrite the essay. What is it about?"

"It's about the corruption of government due to selfish motives," Luc said, still scowling.

"Huh," said Lilou. "Perhaps this experience will give you a whole new perspective to draw upon." She smiled furtively as she turned and went back up the stairs. "I'm going to get dressed," she called behind her. "Then I suggest we all go out and see how Papa could use our help."

Concerned about her planned meetup with Alice in the tunnel at noon, Esme picked up her walkie-talkie from the kitchen windowsill and sent a Morse code message to Alice.

"Alice, do you copy?" Esme tapped out the dashes and dots.

After a few moments, Alice's dashes and dots replied, "Copy."

"Do you have power? We don't."

"No power," replied Alice in Morse code.

"Everyone safe?"

"All good," Alice replied.

"Need to help with cows. Meet later?" Esme messaged.

"Yes," came the reply.

"Why don't you just call each other on the phone?" griped Luc. "Or talk on the walkie-talkies? It would be a whole lot easier."

Knowing it would only be agitating to have any kind of discussion with her disgruntled brother, Esme put on her coat and boots, stretching rubber ice cleats over them from toe to heel, and headed out into the downpour toward the barn.

Disappointed as she was, Esme knew there would be time later to meet up with Alice to make their plans. It gave her something exciting to look forward to.

She was still in awe of the winter scene before her. The icicles were growing longer, the boughs of the trees loomed heavier, and the ground seemed more slick than ever. The power lines stretching across their property sagged with the weight of the ice that was growing in circumference around them.

A truck hauling their generator was pulling off their property. Jérôme waved goodbye and turned toward the barn where Esme was headed. Walking slowly and lost in thought, he appeared weary. Lilou and Luc came out behind Esme, and the family converged just outside the milking barn.

"Let's go in, out of the rain," Jérôme said as he opened the door. They were assaulted by a concentrated stench offensive even to dairy farmers.

"Whoa! Why does it smell so bad?" asked Luc.

"That's ammonia buildup. It's because we haven't cleaned out the gutters to clear the manure and urine from last night and this morning," Jérôme said. "Plus, without the ventilation fans, the air gets stale really fast. It's a problem if the cows have to breathe air like this for too long. Their respiratory tracts could become infected, which could lead to pneumonia."

"Pneumonia?" Luc repeated. "And then what?"

"Well, they either recover, or they die," Jérôme said seriously.

"So what can we do?" asked Lilou.

"We pray the power comes back on soon," Jérôme said. "I was about to run the gutter cleaner before I agreed to loan out the generator."

"Why don't they have their own generators?" Luc asked. "Now our cows could get sick and die because they weren't prepared!"

"Most farmers can't afford a generator large enough for the job. Generators are not easy to come by. I couldn't just let their animals suffer. A productive cow can produce forty-four liters of milk a day. Just imagine the distress of a cow that has not been milked all day, not to mention lactating cows that have not had a drink because everyone has electric well pumps to bring the water up."

"So, what now? Do we need to haul the manure out by wheelbarrow?" Luc asked.

"We'll see what we can get done when we have the generator back. Each of the eighty cows in this barn produces about forty-five kilograms of manure every day. That's four tons of manure per day. I don't know that we could haul that much out if we worked around the clock, even with Henri and Pierre helping. But if we don't get it out, it's going to start overflowing into the stalls and alleys and cause all kinds of problems.

"Right now what I need to do is get ahold of the milk truck to see when they'll be here to empty our tank. If they don't get here by our evening milking, we may have to start dumping milk."

Esme knew that was the same thing as pouring dollars down the drain.

"But that also has to be done when we have the generator because we need electricity to pump the milk out," Jérôme said.

"Why did you lend out our generator?" Luc asked. "We really need it."

"Because I hope they would do the same for me if I were in a bind." Jérôme gave Luc a pat on the back and picked up the phone. Before dialing, he suggested, "What you all could do now is fill the feed mixer with grain and silage, first for the milk cows. We'll feed the heifers and steers after. Luc, you know the mix for the milk cows, right? The ratios are on the side of the grain silo. Be very careful with the ratios because if we get them wrong, it can be costly, and it could make the cows sick."

"Can we say a prayer?" Esme asked timidly.

Jérôme hung up the phone. "That's a wonderful idea," he said. The family joined hands, and Jérôme prayed for the safety of their family, their cows, and their neighbors, and for God's protection over them all.

Jérôme called and scheduled the milk truck to come. Then they went to work.

CHAPTER 5

NATURE'S WAR

It was after ten o'clock that night when Esme finally dropped into bed after working nearly the entire day on the farm with her family. She didn't know it was possible to feel such a degree of exhaustion, but she was thankful her soreness from the fall had continued to disappear as she worked, rather than get worse.

The night felt like it passed in a moment before her maman was nudging her to wake up. "The generator is back," Lilou said. "We need to get the milking and as many other chores done as possible while we have power, so it's all hands on deck."

"What time is it?" It felt like the middle of the night.

"It's five forty-five," Lilou responded. She performed another quick inspection of the bandage on Esme's forehead and then kissed the top of her head. "Get dressed and come out to the barn. Don't forget your ice cleats."

The morning was much the same as the previous night: feeding, milking, and cleaning as fast as they could. They managed to run the gutter cleaners, which hauled out so much excrement that Luc had to take double the usual number of loads to the manure pit. Esme watched with admiration as her brother maneuvered the tractor with impressive skill. She wondered if she would ever be brave enough to learn to do all the things he did.

The milk truck had made it there the night before, after their generator had been returned, so they felt keenly blessed to have an empty cooler tank. Between the cold weather and the intermittent power from the generator, the milk stayed at a safe temperature. That gave them until tomorrow evening before they would need milk pickup again.

The rain was relentless. What had started out beautiful had become burdensome.

Pierre had been unable to make it that morning due to the icy conditions, but Henri came, and the five of them worked tenaciously for four hours. At ten o'clock Jérôme disconnected the generator and drove it over to Brewster, who owned a neighboring farm. They had worked out a rotation with the three farmers sharing the generator: The Errards did their milking at six o'clock in the morning and evening, the Brewsters did theirs at ten o'clock in the morning and evening, and Mr. Fotakis—another nearby dairy farmer—did his milking at two o'clock in the morning and afternoon. It wasn't ideal for anyone, but it was working well enough.

In between milking and cleaning, they did the feeding and anything else they could do to make their next four-hour time slot with the generator most productive. It was exhausting, round-the-clock work. Esme wasn't sure when her parents had slept that night because they were feeding the herd well before the six a.m. milking.

Tuesday passed for Esme in a blur of chores, a nap, more chores, and then nighttime. It seemed they were all in survival mode, subsisting on cold cereal and canned pasta. While they had the generator, everyone was too busy working to take a hot shower, much less eat a hot meal.

Wednesday was more of the same. Esme felt that the freezing rain would never stop. She and Luc had put school on pause because their help was needed on the farm.

The house was filled with the most delightful smell when they walked back in just after ten o'clock, cold, tired, and famished. Lilou had pulled out steaks and ribs from the freezer that were now only partially frozen; placed them in a big pot with carrots, potatoes, herbs, and spices; and let them boil on the electric stove while the generator ran. The family relished the comforting stew together, grateful for a hearty, hot meal.

"Esme, where's your Franken-boom box?" her papa

asked. "Maybe we could turn it on and get some news. The newspaper hasn't been delivered in a couple of days." Esme was happy to put her battery-powered radio to good use. She turned it on, and the family listened as they enjoyed their stew and some orange slices.

They caught the end of an upbeat, cheerful song, which did nothing to relieve the dark circles under their eyes or their aching muscles.

"This is 94.9 Rouge, where you still get your favorite playlist. You can count on us to help you feel good. Now enjoy this favorite by—"

"Change it to CFRA 580, please," Jérôme requested.

Esme switched the radio to AM frequency and turned the dial to 580.

". . . ice rain may continue into Friday, weather reports are now saying. Power is out from Kingston to the northern Ottawa area, and all the way east past Montreal and Sherbrooke. Farther south, parts of New York and a large area of Maine are also affected. That's one hundred eighty-one thousand square kilometers and over four million people without power, folks. As the storm continues, it is difficult to say when power will be restored. The power company has been difficult to reach for commentary. Shelters are set up in each city where people can go to get warm and eat a meal. We encourage those who need the assistance to go to a nearby shelter. The army has supplied cots, and meals and snacks are also being provided. Again, a state of emergency has been declared in these areas. The military is providing assistance where needed. Temperatures are expected to drop this weekend to well below freezing . . ."

Jérôme reached over and shut the radio off.

The phone rang. "Hello? Errard residence." Esme's parents had trained her and Luc when they were very young on how they should answer the phone, and they had answered that way ever since.

"Esme, it's Alice."

"Alice!" she said, thrilled to hear her best friend's voice.

"How are you all doing over there?" Alice asked.

"Fine. Tired, but we're fine. It's just a lot of work, ya know? How are you and your family?"

"We're okay too. Just a little tired of cold canned food and cereal. And tired of the cold in general."

"You should come over! Maman just made a huge pot of stew while we had the generator."

"Tell her whole family to come," Lilou interjected. "We have plenty."

"Maman said your whole family should come over and eat. It's probably a bit warmer here, too, because we have heat while the generator is here," Esme said.

The Giroux family came right over through the tunnel. Esme stepped into her cleated boots and ran to open the cellar door to welcome Alice's family. The tunnel was by far the easiest way to travel between the two homes, especially in this weather.

Alice; her parents, Jacques and Chantal; and her three little sisters—Gisèle, Inés, and Reine—were welcomed warmly into the Errard home. While the three younger girls removed their *tuques*, revealing the wavy red hair they'd inherited from their mother, they all kept their coats on as they sat at the table with hot bowls of stew. Appreciation shone in their six matching pairs of green eyes.

"Wow, this is delicious," Chantal said. She pulled her coat around her stout figure. "Thank you again for having us over. The girls were going a little stir-crazy."

"A little?" Jacques said, rubbing his bald head in feigned disbelief. "*A lot.* A lot stir-crazy! This is a welcome reprieve in more ways than one! Thank you again!" Esme loved Jacques's booming voice and warm charisma, which only seemed enhanced by his brown bushy beard.

"We should have had you all over sooner," Jérôme explained. "We've just been trying to keep up on the farm. It's been all-consuming."

"What can we do to help?" Chantal asked.

"Yes!" Jacques said. "Alice and Esme can entertain the little girls while we help with farm chores."

Esme and Alice grinned at each other.

"It looks like they wouldn't mind." Jérôme chuckled. "If you're really up for it, we could definitely use some extra sets of hands," he said.

"Yes!" Esme exclaimed. She was super excited to have some time with Alice, and she was eager to ask

Alice's little sisters what would be fun to do at a forest adventure camp. She was also thrilled to get a break from farm chores.

When everyone was finished eating, Luc shuffled outside with all the adults while Alice and Esme stayed inside with the little girls.

Esme ran around gathering supplies to keep the girls entertained. First, she grabbed a clipboard with a stack of paper and a pen for taking notes. She also got a large box of crayons from their cupboard full of art supplies. Remembering a portable propane heater she had seen in the cellar, she hurried out and brought it in. Without the generator it was getting chilly in the house, so Esme was delighted to provide warmth for her small guests. She set it on the kitchen table and turned it up as high as it would go. The heat that poured out of it felt luxurious!

"Okay." Esme took charge with the clipboard in hand. "Alice and I are your adventure camp directors! We want to know what fun things you would like to do at a forest adventure camp."

The girls—nine, six, and four—raised their hands exuberantly.

"You are going to draw your ideas on your paper with these crayons," Alice instructed. "The best ideas will be added to the adventure camp schedule. Ready . . . go!"

Esme and Alice smiled at each other as the three little girls set to work, crayons to paper. Four-year-old Reine drew some grass, then stopped and looked up at the camp directors, a concerned look on her face.

"What's the matter, Reine?" Alice asked.

"Can you help me draw a skunk?" Reine requested sweetly, her red curls framing her round face.

"A skunk? Why do you want to draw a skunk?" Alice asked.

"Because they're cute. I want to catch one at adventure camp," explained Reine innocently.

Esme and Alice giggled, but Alice obliged and drew a skunk for her little sister.

While the three little campers drew page after page of ideas, the camp directors drew maps and ideas of their own. They'd been working on plans for an hour or so when Inés, the six-year-old, complained, "My head hurts."

Lilou came in right then to check on the girls. Spotting the heater, she rushed over and shut it off, then threw open the back door. Her face grim, she raced to the front door, throwing it wide open as well. She sped back to the girls, a look of fear spread across her face.

"What is it, Maman?" Esme asked. "Why did you turn off our heater? You're making the house cold again."

"Are you all feeling okay?" Lilou took each girl by the shoulders, her stricken face searching their eyes. They looked back at her questioningly.

"Who brought this heater in here?" Lilou asked.

"I did," Esme said hesitantly. "So we could get warm."

Lilou seemed frightened. "Sweetheart, you can't have a gas heater indoors. It could cause carbon monoxide poisoning. People die from that."

Esme gasped, panicked at the thought of causing harm—or worse—to her friends!

"Are we going to die?" Inés asked solemnly.

"No, no. No one is going to die. Sorry, I was . . . It just scared me, that's all. Let's go outside for a minute and get some fresh air." Soon, Inés's head was feeling much better.

Esme felt sick inside. *What if Maman had not come when she did? What if . . .* She choked back tears, considering what might have happened.

Later that night the Errard family had a serious discussion about the dangers of certain heat sources in unventilated areas.

"You have to have a window open for fresh oxygen to flow in if you are going to have a gas-powered heat source in the house," Esme's papa said after explaining what might have happened if her maman had not come in the house when she did.

Tears streamed down Esme's face. "I'm sorry. I was just trying to help," she cried.

"Oh, sweetheart, we know. It's not your fault. This is something we should have taught you before. You're not in trouble or anything. And now you know." He tousled her hair and then kissed her softly on the head. "Why don't you head to bed? We could all use the rest."

Esme trudged toward her bedroom and changed quickly in the frigid room. Her cold pajamas made her shiver, so she jumped into bed, pulling her heavy patchwork quilt around her shoulders. She peered out her window.

The ice rain had not stopped falling for three solid days now. The trees had become so burdened with ice that they were literally cracking under the weight. *This must be what war sounds like*, Esme thought fearfully as she wrapped herself more tightly in her quilt. The splintering of hundreds of trees was deafening, like a militia of shotguns, as branches buckled and trunks gave way to the tons of ice that clung mercilessly to their boughs, bringing them crashing to the ground. She feared the worst for the neighboring maple farm, her heart aching for the Giroux family.

She could see explosions in the distance that morphed the whole skyline into an electric-blue strobe light, followed by a loud *BOOM*, several smaller *booms*, and sprays of orange sparks that resembled fireworks. "Are those transformer boxes?" she questioned aloud, alarmed. The cows bellowing in the barn were so loud she could hear them from the house. Suddenly, there was an earsplitting *CRRRRACK* and *POP* right outside her window as the ice-laden electrical line by their house snapped in two. Esme jumped out of bed and ran through the dark hallway to her parents' room.

CHAPTER 6

ICE-LOCKED

Esme overslept on Thursday morning. When she walked outside at dawn to help with chores, their property looked like a war zone. Power poles had toppled to the ground like bowling pins, many broken clean off, others angled precariously this way and that. The power lines were strewn around like threatening silvery snakes with blackened cores. Ice-laden tree branches littered the wintry ground. Branches that were once the width of a pencil were now the size of a broomstick due to the layers of ice that had frozen around them. Massive chunks of ice had slid off the barn roof and lay in jagged heaps beneath the eaves. Despite the rain, there was an odd smell that lingered in the air, later explained to Esme as ozone: the result of intense heat and energy associated with electrical discharge. In the distance the frequent groan and cracking of trees surrendering to the weight of their icy shackles could still be heard.

It wasn't until after the morning chores were done that the Errard family realized the telephone service was out.

"Phone line is dead," Jérôme announced stiffly as he came in from the barn. "I was going to schedule the milk pickup for tonight, but I can't get through." He picked up Esme's boom box and switched the radio on.

The family listened as they sat around the table, enjoying hot stew again. Lilou had clamped the lid on the pot and set it outside in a snowbank to stay cold. While the generator was running each morning and evening at six, she put it back on the stove, added more water and ingredients, and let it cook while they all did the barn chores. A hot meal was served twice a day that way. Otherwise, it was crackers and cheese (hummus for Esme), peanut butter sandwiches, canned beans, or canned pasta, which Esme didn't think was too bad at all.

". . . storm has pulled down thirty-five *thousand* telephone poles," the radio personality broadcasted. "You heard that number correctly: thirty-five thousand telephone poles. It's even destroying transmission towers. The massive steel pylons are buckling under the weight of thousands of tons of ice. Over one thousand transmission towers are down. Folks, we are talking over three thousand kilometers of telephone lines down. The power company is now reporting that some people may go weeks without electricity as crews work around the clock to restore power to cities, businesses, and homes. That's right—it could be weeks, possibly a month in some places. Military or police personnel may knock at your door. Do not be alarmed. They have been instructed to check on homes and make sure people are okay. Unless there is a wood-burning stove in the home, residents without power are being urged to make their way to a shelter. However, outside travel can be very dangerous due to fallen trees and power lines. Choose your route wisely and carefully. Crews are working to remove the hazards. Please be patient. Do not drive over downed power lines because there is no way to tell if they are live when they are lying in the street."

Jérôme turned off the radio. "Weeks?" he said, incredulous.

The mood in the house was solemn. Jérôme shook his head. "How long can we keep doing this?" he sighed. The lines around his mouth and on his forehead appeared to have grown deeper in the past few days.

Lilou's face was in her hands. When she lifted her head, her eyes were wet. "We have got to see if we can find another generator," she said. "We cannot go on like this for weeks." Lilou's exhaustion was evident as she wept. "And now we can't even call anyone?"

Esme picked up her walkie-talkie and sent a Morse code to Alice: "Do you copy?" Esme waited thirty seconds and then sent the code again. "Do you copy?"

"Copy," Alice coded back.

"Does your phone work?" Esme asked.

"Yes," came Alice's reply.

"Alice said their phone still works!" Esme announced.

"That could be helpful," Jérôme said.

"How about I go over and use their phone to schedule the milk truck?" Lilou suggested. "I'd like to check on them anyway. The temperature in here is cold. I can't imagine how frigid it must be there for those little girls."

"Esme, can you ask Alice if we could use their phone?" Jérôme asked. He turned to Lilou. "See if you can schedule the truck between six and nine tonight; the earlier the better."

Esme sent another Morse code to Alice. A reply was quick to follow.

"She said we can! Can I go with you, Maman?"

"Of course." Lilou quickly dried her tears on the back of her sleeve. "Let's take a pot of this stew over for them." She pulled a clean pot from the cupboard and ladled a generous amount of stew into it, placing a lid on top.

"On our way," Esme sent to Alice.

After bundling up, Esme grabbed a flashlight and headed toward the cellar. Lilou followed her with the pot of hot stew.

"Do you think they have lost a lot of maple trees?" Esme asked as they walked together through the tunnel.

"I don't know. I guess we are about to find out," Lilou said. "We need to count our blessings that we have not lost any cattle. We've heard from the milk-truck driver that some farmers have been losing cattle to pneumonia and infections. Another farmer's barn roof collapsed from the ice load and killed his entire herd. I can't imagine . . ."

Esme could tell that the door on the other end had been opened because of the soft light that filtered into the gloom of the tunnel. As she and her mother ascended the steps to the opening, Alice was there waiting, but something was off about her best friend. Her usual vibrance was replaced by a slack expression and stooped posture.

Then Esme saw it—the devastation of the trees all around them. Trees that once stood tall and majestic were now bowed and broken under the tyranny of ice that clutched onto their branches. Like bones scattered on the forest floor, icy tree limbs littered the frozen ground.

"Oh, Alice," Esme said softly.

"Papa said to hurry into the house. It's not safe to linger here . . . as you can see," Alice said grimly. A groaning tree echoed the warning.

The three of them hurried to the back door of the Giroux home.

"Chantal . . ." Lilou said, her words breaking off into an expression of deep concern as they walked into the house. Chantal's eyes were red and puffy, but she managed a thin smile as Lilou handed her the pot of hot stew.

"Thank you very much. Girls, do you want to come have some nice warm stew that Mrs. Errard brought over?" Chantal called out to her daughters.

"Stew!" one of them shouted, and Gisèle, Inés, and Reine—all bundled in coats and hats—hurried over to the dining room table.

"Who knew hot stew would ever be so exciting?" Chantal said with a good-natured chuckle. "Would you like some, Alice?" she turned to her daughter, who was standing next to Esme.

"I'm not hungry," Alice said quietly. "Thank you."

"Where is Jacques?" Lilou asked.

"He is outside with his chain saw, trying to clear fallen trees from our driveway and the road. But I will save him some stew. He will be very happy," Chantal said. "Thank you for bringing it."

"Of course," replied Lilou. "It's so cold in here. Our house isn't a lot warmer, but maybe your family should come stay with us for a while?" She noticed a digital clock on the counter that also showed the temperature in Celsius and Fahrenheit. It read 4 °C/39 °F. "Is this the temperature inside the house?"

"Yes," said Chantal abashedly. "Thank you, but we have decided to go to the shelter at the junior high in town. Once Jacques finishes clearing the drive, we will go."

Esme looked at Alice, surprised and a little disappointed. "How long will you be gone?" Esme asked.

Alice shrugged her shoulders in response.

"I'm really sorry about your trees," Esme said. "Will you still be able to get sap from them this spring?"

"We don't know yet," Alice said, her voice heavy with the loss and the unknown. "It's still too dangerous to go through and see what damage has been done. Trees are still breaking. I think that's one of the reasons we need to go. It's too sad for Papa to hear all his trees being destroyed. They've been in the family since his great-grandparents."

Esme noticed Chantal's lip quiver as she looked down, hands wrapped tightly around a mug.

"What can we do?" Lilou asked compassionately.

"There is nothing to do, for now anyway," Chantal answered. "That is why we decided it is better for us at the shelter, where it is warm and there is food. This soup is wonderful. It is the best thing you could do for us now. Thank you," she said sincerely.

"Is it okay if I use your phone for just a minute?" Lilou asked.

"Yes, yes, of course," Chantal said, motioning to the phone on the counter.

As Lilou made a call to arrange for milk pickup, Esme turned to Alice. "Is the treehouse okay?"

"I don't know. I'm afraid to go look. I don't want to know," Alice said.

"What about the sugar shack?" Esme asked hesitantly.

"Papa said that has taken some damage. He's not sure yet how much," Alice replied.

The feeling in the home was melancholic. Esme wished there were something she could do. She wrapped her arms around Alice. "I will miss you. Maybe the shelter will be fun. I want to hear all about it, okay?"

Alice nodded, a reluctant smile inching across her lips.

"Who will I send Morse code to now?" Esme asked. "I might have to teach Luc."

"Don't you dare! I'll be back soon!"

Ah, that was the Alice Esme knew.

CHAPTER 7

DEEPENING TRIALS

After chores were done on Friday morning, Esme and her family turned on the radio during breakfast, as had become habit. Lilou had taken time to make pancakes and sausage, a welcome departure from the endless hodgepodge stew that had become slightly less appetizing with each serving—and slightly more mysterious as meats and vegetables long buried in the depths of the freezer were introduced.

". . . and as the ice storm continues across parts of Ontario and southern Quebec," the broadcaster announced, "the coming weekend offers no reprieve to millions of Canadians still without power due to the worst ice storm in recorded history. The weekend will, according to weather reports, bring a severe dip in temperature, making conditions dangerously cold for those with no heat in their homes. Authorities are strongly urging all residents without a source of heat, such as a wood-burning stove or fireplace, to evacuate immediately to a shelter or locations outside the outage area. Warnings have been issued regarding the use of gas heat sources inside confined spaces without proper ventilation."

At this, Esme's cheeks flushed hot, remembering the propane heater she had brought into the house a couple of days ago.

The radio announcer continued, "A high number of people have been admitted to local hospitals with carbon monoxide poisoning, which has been the leading cause of death during the storm so far, with six known deaths from carbon monoxide poisoning and five known deaths from hypothermia. Again, due to the impending temperature drop tonight well below freezing, if you do not have a safe source of heat in your home, you are urged to immediately evacuate . . ."

"Are we going to evacuate?" Esme asked.

"No, sweetie," her papa said. "Farmers cannot evacuate. We have animals to care for and responsibilities that must be attended to no matter the weather."

"Speaking of responsibilities," Lilou turned to Esme and Luc, "you two need to be doing something for school every day. I am not able to do it with you for now, but I would like you to at least read each day for an hour."

Luc groaned, but Esme was thrilled to have permission—even instruction—to sit and read for an hour when keeping up with chores demanded such constant attention. Reading, for her, was like a mini vacation, an escape into another world where she could experience life through someone else. Sometimes she read to simply quench her thirst for knowledge on a particular subject.

"Can it be anything?" Esme asked.

"Within reason," her mother said, eyeing her suspiciously. "Did you have something in mind?"

"Uh . . ." Esme unzipped her coat and reached inside apprehensively. As she was cleaning the stalls that morning, she had spotted a booklet that sparked her interest. It had been resting on a shelf next to various farm implements. She had planned to read it when she could find the time and then return it, sure no one would notice—not that there was anything wrong with reading it, but she was certain her family would think she was odd for doing so. Esme pulled the booklet hesitantly from her coat, her whole family watching her with curious stares.

"The generator instruction book?" Lilou asked. "That's what you want to read?"

"A manual?" Luc snorted. "You want to read a manual?" He got up from the table, his eyebrows lifted as he carried his plate to the sink.

"If that's what you want to read, sweetie, you go right ahead," Jérôme encouraged. "In fact, you could sit with me in the tractor while I do the feed, and we'll crank up the heat so you can be cozy and warm."

Esme's face lit up, elated. "Right now?"

"Let me just take those butterfly strips off your forehead, Esme," Lilou piped up. "They're starting to come off on their own, and it looks like you've got a nice scab formed over the wound."

Esme held her breath as her mother gently pulled off the adhesives. Thankful to be done with the head bandage, she jumped up from her seat and ran to get her boots and coat.

"All right. Let's go," her papa said as he put his cowboy hat on his head, pulling the brim down over his forehead. He gave Lilou a kiss and thanked her for the satisfying breakfast.

With Alice gone, taking with her the excitement of planning their adventure camp, the next best thing for Esme was getting cozy and warm with a book in the tractor with her papa.

Jérôme pulled up to the silos and hopped out to mix the cattle feed. He didn't ask Esme to help with anything, and she didn't feel guilty for not helping since she was "doing school." She read the "Safety Instructions and Introduction" in the manual. But the part she was most excited to read and spent the most time studying was "Electrical Connections," which she found fascinating, from the plug kit to the circuit panels to the wiring diagram.

After nearly an hour of reading in the warm tractor cab, Esme's eyelids began to droop, and drowsiness crept over her in an inviting wave, beckoning her to the deep waters of sleep. Jérôme opened the cab door and hopped back into his seat, a draft of cold air whooshing in with him, jolting her out of sleep's grasp.

"Don't you get tired, Papa?" Esme asked languidly.

Her father smiled, his tanned, rugged face thick with five days of whiskers, the creases growing deeper around his eyes. "What do you mean?"

"You work on the farm all day long and at night too. Don't you get tired?"

"Sure, I'm tired a lot of the time, especially lately," he said.

"How do you keep going?" Esme asked. "I mean, when all you want to do is sleep?"

"I try to rest when I can," he replied, stifling an involuntary yawn. "But when there's more work to be done and rest has to wait, I think of you and Luc and Maman. You three are the reason I do all of this." He smiled at Esme. "The thought of you helps me keep going. And then, when it all feels like way too much, and sometimes it does, I pray." He paused and thought for a moment. "I pray and ask God to give me the strength to keep going and the guidance to be smarter about how I do things. There are a lot of ways to do something. But God knows the best way. So I try to listen and pay attention to what He tells me."

"How does He tell you?" Esme asked.

"It depends. Sometimes it's an idea or a thought.

Sometimes it's a friend or neighbor who teaches me something. It can be an article I happen to see in a magazine or even some creative burst of inspiration. One time I got an idea at the hardware store that turned out to be an answer to prayer."

"Ah, so that's why you love the hardware store so much," Esme said. "You find God there."

"Yeah, I try to convince your maman that the hardware store is a place of inspiration." A facetious grin spread across Papa's handsome face.

Shortly after six o'clock that evening, the generator was returned on schedule. With a renewed interest in how it worked, Esme watched attentively as Jérôme and Henri plugged it in and made sure it was grounded by connecting a copper wire from the generator to a rod driven deep into the ground. Then Luc refueled it with gasoline and turned it on. The machine roared to life, bringing heavenly light to the house and barns.

As forecasted, the temperature was steadily dropping, yet the rain continued because of the layer of warm air that hovered in the atmosphere above. Like a parachute with no time to open, the rain didn't quite have time to transform into fluffy snow for a soft landing but fell fast and froze solid on contact. In addition to the icy rain that night, lightning flashed across the skies, and thunder rumbled all around them. Esme generally relished the spectacle of a good lightning and thunder storm, but recalling the frightening explosions of power boxes two days prior, and working outside in such dire conditions, she found that the thunderstorm felt foreboding and angry. Her body shivered.

Jérôme, Henri, Esme, and Luc had just walked into the barn when the lights went out. The generator's roar changed abruptly to a sputter and a cough. The comfort of the light was immediately snatched away and replaced with dread—no lights, no heat, and no way to milk and water the cattle, much less cook a meal for themselves or even take a shower.

They hurried back out to the generator, which sat on a concrete pad under an awning next to the freestall barn where the heifers were bedded and fed.

Maybe I can do something to help, Esme thought. She had, after all, just been reading the manual for this particular generator. She flipped to the "Troubleshooting" section in her mind.

While Jérôme and Henri examined the motor with a flashlight, Esme ticked off the various issues she had read about that may cause a generator to malfunction.

Lilou came hurrying over to the barn to see what was happening.

"Our problem is we have no output voltage, right?" Esme took charge. "Check the circuit breaker."

"Circuit breaker is fine," Jérôme said.

"Are the receptacles defective?" Esme asked.

"What's that?" Henri questioned.

Esme pointed out the receptacles.

"They seem to be okay," her papa replied.

"Are there any loose wires or connections in the control box?" Esme asked.

"Where is the control box?" he asked.

"It's this right here," Esme pointed out. They checked the wires together.

"If it's none of those things, then it's either the rotor or the stator, and that's not good. Those parts have to be repaired or replaced," Esme stated.

Jérôme, Henri, Lilou, and Luc all stared dumbfounded at Esme.

"The good news is, our daughter is a genius," Jérôme said. "The bad news is, I think she's right. There's no way this generator will run with a broken rotor or stator."

"What are we going to do?" Lilou asked, her eyebrows drawn together, the circles under her eyes more prominent than ever. "Without this generator, three farms are unable to do their milking." She began pacing in tight circles, breathing deeply.

"The generator wasn't on long enough for the well pump to draw up water to the troughs," Luc said anxiously.

In the milk barn, the cows bellowed, their udders full—and the whole herd would soon be bawling for water.

CHAPTER 8

ENERGY QUEST

"Henri," Jérôme said, "I need you to take the truck and go tell Brewster and Mr. Fotakis that our generator is broken. We need them to help come up with a solution. All of us were depending on this generator, and they need to know it won't be available for their next milking tonight."

"But I don't speak English," Henri said. "Do they speak any French?"

"A little." Jérôme thought for a moment. "Luc, you go with Henri. Your English is good." Jérôme paused again, thinking under pressure. "Actually, I'll come too. Then the three of us need to go in search of a generator. I'll need your help to get it into the truck when we find one."

"It's almost seven o'clock," said Luc. "By the time we tell them, it will be seven thirty. Where are we going to find a generator?"

"I'm not sure, but we can't do anything here without one, so we have to try," Jérôme said decidedly. "Will you two be okay here?" he asked Lilou and Esme.

"We'll be fine," Lilou assured him. "Drive safe. Hurry back."

Esme and Lilou went back in the house and, with nothing else to do, lit a few candles and turned on the "Franken-boom box," as Jérôme called it.

". . . and that's not the only danger," the radio voice said. "Water utility companies have issued a warning not to drink tap water due to water purification systems being down and unable to filter the water. Any tap water must be boiled before consumption . . ."

"We can't even get water from our tap," Esme fretted. "Not when our well pump is electric."

"Yeah, and how are we supposed to boil the water on our electric stove?" Lilou asked the radio, clearly annoyed, stress and sleep deprivation taking their toll.

". . . once again, this is News Talk 580 CFRA, where we keep you informed. This segment is reserved for you, our listeners, to call in and tell us what you are experiencing with the storm. A woman called in yesterday to tell us she has five little kids at home and no water. After her story aired, five people showed up at her home with jugs of water. Another caller said a huge tree had fallen on his house. Within the hour a number of people came with chain saws to remove the tree. Canadians are pulling together to help each other out! Call in and tell us your story! Our number is 1-800-580-CFRA. If you have called in previously and people stepped up to help you, call us back and let us know. Again, the number is 1-800-580-CFRA."

Lilou and Esme, despite both still wearing their coats and *tuques*, wrapped themselves up in blankets and huddled on the couch for warmth as they listened.

"This is CFRA; welcome! You're on the air," the radio host said.

"Uh, yes, hello," a man stammered with a foreign accent. "Our baby had heart surgery a month ago. She has to have medication that requires refrigeration."

"Ah, yes! I remember you," the radio host said. "You had to throw away the expensive medication when the power went out because the medication had not been kept at the right temperature."

"That's right. We did not have any more medication, and the baby needed a dose every six hours. It was already nine o'clock at night when we realized we needed a new bottle of medicine. She would need another dose at midnight. We didn't know what to do, so we called in here to ask for help. Just a minute later, we got a call from a pharmacist in Ottawa who invited us to meet that night at her pharmacy to fill our daughter's prescription. We were able to get the medicine! We are very grateful."

"Wow, that's quite the story! This is what we love to hear: people pulling together to get help and to give help. Sometimes we need help but don't know where to turn, and other times we want to help but don't know what is needed. That is exactly the purpose of this segment, so we can connect people who need help to the people who can meet those needs. Hello, welcome to CFRA. You're on the air," the radio host said.

"Hi, my name's Myra. I heard on your station that a local shelter was looking for volunteers to help make and serve food. Well, here I was sitting all alone in my cold house, feeling sorry for myself, when I heard that caller. I used to work as the head chef in a restaurant, so I thought, 'I can do that.' And I did! I went to the shelter, and they put me to work. These have been some of the longest days of my life, but I don't believe I've ever been happier! And I'm warm!"

"Warm from the inside out, it sounds like, eh?" the radio host said.

"That's exactly right!" the caller said. "There's a warmth that comes from helping people that can't be found in any other way."

"That's beautiful. That's why we're here, folks. If you are in need of help, give us a call at 1-800 . . ."

"Maman!" Esme exclaimed suddenly. "What if we call in and tell them we need a generator?"

"Everyone could use a generator," Lilou said. "They are in short supply. I really don't know if calling the radio station would help—especially for the size of generator we need for the farm. When we started loaning out our generator, your father even checked with the military post to see if they had another. They said they had ordered some that were late in arriving. All they could do was put our name on a waiting list."

"But it couldn't hurt," Esme said eagerly. "We could try!"

Lilou eyed Esme doubtfully. "How would we even make a call?"

"Oh, yeah. No phone line," Esme remembered. "And Alice's family has gone to a shelter." Her shoulders slumped disconsolately.

"What if . . ." Lilou said.

Esme perked up, "Yeah?"

"What if we drive to the gas station and use the pay phone?"

Filled with hope once again, Esme said, "Yes! And can we get a doughnut while we're there?"

"Sounds good to me!" Lilou said.

They turned off the radio and went outside into the freezing rain. When they got to the car, they were hit with a stark realization: Their four-door sedan was completely encased in three or four inches of solid ice, unlike the truck, which had been parked under a carport attached to the barn. Esme ran her fingers across the smooth, lumpy surface, amazed by the transformation. By this time it was after eight o'clock in the evening. They could hear the cows bellowing loudly in the barn, desperate to be milked and crying for a drink of water.

The gas station was only about five miles away, but the challenge of maneuvering on slippery roads was intimidating. Now seeing their ice-encrusted car, Esme realized she and her maman might not even get the chance to try. They could not open the doors to start the car and turn on defrost; the handles were completely iced over, as were all the doors, and the rain was not letting up.

With nothing else to do, Esme and Lilou began chipping away at the ice, first with an ice scraper—completely useless—then with kitchen knives, which were not any better, and finally with hammers, which they carefully used to tap on the ice until brittle chunks cracked and fell away.

Esme worked on freeing the driver's door while Lilou worked on deicing the windshield. After thirty minutes, their outer layers were drenched from the rain, and they had only been somewhat successful at removing ice, when headlights came up the driveway. They weren't her papa's headlights. As the vehicle approached, Esme wondered who would come to their farm this late in the freezing rain during a power outage.

"Alice!" Esme shouted as the Girouxs' gray van became recognizable in the dark. A back door slid open, and Alice hopped out, followed by her little sisters.

"What are you doing?" Alice asked.

"I was going to ask you the same thing!" Esme responded as the two girls hugged.

“We brought some food from the shelter,” Alice said, smiling. “It’s actually pretty good.”

“Yeah, it’s teriyaki chicken with sticky rice,” Gisèle said happily.

“We brought cooked broccoli, too,” said Inés. “I don’t usually like broccoli, but it’s good with the sauce from the chicken.”

“And grapes!” Reine piped up cheerfully.

Esme’s stomach rumbled, and she realized she had not eaten dinner. She suddenly felt famished, and the warm meal sounded delectable.

“Thank you for coming,” Lilou said, giving Chantal a hug. Esme could see the tension on her mother’s face loosening with the happy energy brought by their neighbors.

“Can we help?” Jacques asked, looking askance at the hammers in Esme’s and Lilou’s hands.

“Uh, let’s get you all inside, out of the rain,” Lilou insisted.

The Giroux family filed into the soft glowing light of the candlelit kitchen and set the paper bags with the warm meal on the dining table.

“Thank you,” Lilou said as they opened the bags and began dishing out the food. “This looks delicious. We were planning to go to a pay phone at the Esso.”

“Yeah, we are going to call into the radio station and tell them we need a generator,” Esme said.

“Where are Jérôme and Luc?” Chantal asked.

"You said you need a generator?" Jacques asked. "I thought you had one."

Lilou breathed out a heavy sigh. "Our generator broke earlier this evening. The cows have not been milked yet."

"That would explain the noise coming from the barn," Alice said.

"Papa and Luc and Henri went to tell the farmers we've been sharing with and to try to find a generator," Esme explained.

"We can give you a ride," Chantal offered. "You can come to our house and use the phone. We should have given you a key! I don't know why I didn't think of that before," she added regretfully.

"You had your own worries," Lilou said, her weariness obvious. "We would love to use your phone, thank you." She turned to Esme. "Would you like to stay here with Alice and her sisters and have some dinner while I go?"

"Yes, but . . ." Esme looked down.

"What is it?" Lilou asked.

"I think the time when you can call in and ask for help might be over by now," Esme said, dismayed.

"That's okay. I can still try," Lilou said, forcing a smile for Esme's sake. "What else can we do?"

"I'll stay here with the children while you ladies go over to the house," Jacques offered.

After dishing up a generous helping of sticky rice, sweet-smelling chicken, and tender broccoli, Esme asked the Giroux family if they would join her.

"Oh, we already ate at the shelter," Alice said.

"How about joining me in prayer, then?" Esme asked, and they agreed. "Dear God," she prayed, her head bowed and fingers clasped earnestly together. "Thank You for this wonderful meal. Thank You for our dear friends who brought it. Please, God, help us find a generator so that our cows don't have to suffer anymore. Amen."

Esme believed she had never eaten anything so satisfying as the teriyaki chicken and broccoli. Her heart was filled as full as her belly by the renewed hope and energy the Girouxs brought with their thoughtful visit. She was nearly finished eating when headlights appeared in the driveway.

"Papa, Luc, and Henri are back!" Esme exclaimed.

When the two men and Luc walked through the back door, shoulders slumped and expressions somber, Esme knew immediately they had not been successful in finding a generator.

Before anyone could exchange news, another set of lights came up the drive. A moment later, Chantal burst through the back door, out of breath, a hand clutching her chest, as she exclaimed, "Our basement is flooded!"

CHAPTER 9

CLINGING TO HOPE

"Where's Maman?" Esme asked, worry rising in her throat.

"The sump pump!" Jacques was up and crossing the room to the back door. "I didn't think it would flood in these freezing temperatures!"

"Where's Maman?" Esme asked again as Alice's parents rushed out the back door, pushing past Jérôme, Henri, and Luc in their race to their running vehicle.

"Wasn't she here with you?" Jérôme asked, staring after Jacques and Chantal in confusion. "I thought the Girouxs went to a shelter."

"Maman!" Reine screamed, running to the back door in pursuit of Chantal.

"Reine, stay here," Alice blurted, hurrying to grab her little sister before she fled the home. "Maman and Papa will be back. We're waiting for them here."

Reine began to cry. It was likely past her bedtime,

Esme surmised, her mind whirring in the chaos as she tried to process everything happening all at once.

"What's a sump pump?" Luc asked, nonchalantly strolling past his surprised father and the crying girl and dishing himself a big bowl of chicken, rice, and broccoli.

"Where did your mother go?" Esme's father asked, now studying the scene in the kitchen.

"She went with Mrs. Giroux to make a phone call at their house. She's calling into CFRA to ask for a generator," Esme said. She explained that their neighbors had come to bring food from the shelter.

"What's a sump pump?" Luc repeated, stuffing his mouth full of food.

Alice, Gisèle, and Inés were still trying in vain to comfort Reine, who was crying inconsolably.

Henri had followed Luc into the kitchen to get food, and now he raised his voice so Luc could hear him over the wailing child. "It's a pump that pulls water out of a drainage area under a basement. If the drainage area gets full and the pump doesn't do its job, water will seep into the basement from the ground up."

"Does it run on electricity?" Esme asked loudly.

"Most of them do," Henri spoke out. "Theirs must not have battery backup."

"Why is she asking the radio station for a generator?" Jérôme practically shouted, confused.

"I'm going to help with the basement," Henri bellowed.

"Go through the tunnel!" Luc hollered with his mouth still full. "It's a lot easier!"

"The radio station has a segment where you can call in and say what you need and people help you," Esme explained matter-of-factly.

"Wait! I'm coming with you," Jérôme said as Henri walked out the back door. "Luc, come along. Hopefully, your mother will still be there."

Luc shoveled the last two bites into his mouth all at once, grabbed a flashlight, and scrambled after his father.

With the men gone, Esme's full attention turned toward trying to help distract the distraught four-year-old with a puppet. It was beginning to work when Lilou walked through the door, just minutes after the others had left.

"What's the matter, dear Reine?" Lilou cooed, scooping the four-year-old up the way only a mother can and holding her close to quiet her cries. She turned to Esme. "Where's Papa?"

"He just left to go help at the Girouxs'," Esme said. "I think they went through the tunnel. He was hoping to find you! How did you get back?"

"Chantal just dropped me off."

"Did you get through to the radio station?" Esme really wanted to know.

"Yes. I didn't get on the air, but they took down our name, as well as Brewster's and Mr. Fotakis's, since we all need generators to complete milking. I also decided to call my brother. I told him about our situation, and he said my uncle has a large generator. I called him, and Uncle Hugo is on his way with one now that we can use for the night."

"He is on his way? How long will it take him to get here?" Esme couldn't believe a generator was on its way!

"About forty-five minutes on normal roads. Could be a lot longer, depending on road conditions."

Esme looked at the clock on the wall. It was nine thirty. Uncle Hugo could possibly arrive with the generator around ten fifteen.

"Does Papa know?" Esme asked.

"No, I was hoping he would be here and I could tell him! Maybe I'll run back through the tunnel," Lilou said, setting the calmed Reine next to Alice.

"Should we come help with the basement?" Alice asked.

Lilou stopped from her hasty retreat and turned toward the five girls staring at her while still bundled in their coats and hats in the chill of the house, the candlelight flickering across their faces.

"We are going to need someone to be here when Uncle Hugo arrives," Lilou said. "Can the girls stay here with you, Esme?"

Esme nodded in agreement. "But how will we let you know when Uncle Hugo gets here?"

"I know!" Alice said. "When you get back to my

house, turn on my walkie-talkie. It's on the mantle above the fireplace. We'll tell you when your uncle arrives."

"Great idea!" Lilou said cheerily. "But please don't use Morse code!"

Giggles filled the dimly lit room. The dulcet tones of laughter were music to Esme's ears.

It's so good to see Maman happy again, Esme thought, relishing her mother's genuine smile.

As the back door was opened, the cacophony of noise from the barn echoed through the frigid night, carrying with it the burdensome weight of miserable cattle that would hopefully lift soon.

Hang on, cows, Esme thought. *Help is coming!* She paused and said a quick, silent prayer of gratitude that her simple plea for help to find a generator had been answered. She prayed that Uncle Hugo would arrive safely and efficiently.

While their family members worked to rescue the Girouxs' basement from water damage, Esme, Alice, Gisèle, and Inés passed the time playing a card game by candlelight, waiting and watching for Uncle Hugo.

"How are things going over there?" Lilou's voice chirped across Esme's walkie-talkie.

"Hi, Maman. We are fine. What is happening over there? Over," Esme replied. She was serious about walkie-talkie etiquette.

"They had a couple of inches of water across the basement," Lilou reported. "The guys have been taking buckets of water from the sump pit, carrying them upstairs and dumping them outside, while Chantal and I have been sweeping the water across the floor to the drain. They are going to have to replace the carpet and probably the baseboards, but hopefully not much else is ruined."

"Is our house going to flood too?" Esme asked, concerned. "Over."

"Well, that's one good thing about not having a basement. We don't have to worry about flooding in the house. But we will want to keep an eye on the cellar," Lilou said. "How are all the girls doing?"

"Fine. Reine is sound asleep on the couch," Esme chuckled. "Over."

"Oh, that's good," Lilou said. "She was so tired. Contact us when Uncle Hugo gets there, okay?"

"You got it. Over and out," Esme said, setting the walkie-talkie down on the kitchen counter.

About fifteen minutes later, headlights came up the drive.

"Come in!" Esme spoke into the walkie-talkie. "Maman! I think he's here! Uncle Hugo. Well, somebody is here." Esme was suddenly a little nervous because, although he lived just forty-five minutes away, she wasn't particularly familiar with Uncle Hugo, as he was her mother's uncle. She had seen him at family reunions before and thought she would recognize him, but she was uncertain. What if it were actually someone else, not Uncle Hugo? She looked at the clock. It was ten thirty-five.

"Okay, we are heading back right now," Lilou said.

Esme felt nervous with no back porch light to illuminate the visitors at the door. She cautiously opened the door a crack and called out, "Hello? Who's there?"

"It's Hugo," a gruff voice called back.

Esme quickly slipped on her boots. "I'll be right back," she said to Alice and her sisters, who continued with their card game.

It took longer than expected for Esme to make her way safely across the slippery yard. The adults had already set the generator on the concrete pad next to the barn. Uncle Hugo was wearing a baseball cap, jeans, and a heavy leather coat. Esme recognized him as the uncle who teasingly threatened to toss the kids into the pool at their reunion two years ago. His warm smile put her at ease. He and her parents were looking at how to hook the generator up to the pole switch. The cows were making such a distressed ruckus that they could not hear each other speak without shouting.

"The connectors are different for your generator than they are for ours," Jérôme said.

"Yeah, I don't have a pole switch," Uncle Hugo replied. "I had to have my electrician hook it up straight to the panel box."

Jérôme's shoulders slumped. He rubbed one eye, took off his cowboy hat, and ran a hand through his hair, taking in a deep breath and letting it out slowly. He looked at his wife. "I don't know if we can find an electrician this late at night."

"What time is it?" Lilou asked.

"Quarter to eleven," he said. He looked down, rubbing the back of his neck.

Esme moved closer to the generator. She examined the control box closely. "Turn off the branch breakers and the main power breaker," she said. "Henri, can you grab a screwdriver and remove the front panel of the breaker box to the milking barn?"

"What are you doing, Esme?" her papa asked.

"I think I can wire this up," she said confidently. "But I need some supplies. Didn't our generator come with a wiring kit? I thought I saw a bag of wires and stuff next to the manual in your workshop," she said to her father.

"I think it's still there," he mused. "We didn't need all that with our pole switch."

Esme ran inside the barn. It didn't take her long to find the dust-covered kit, along with some gloves, electrical tape, and wire cutters.

"You're not really going to let a child do this, are you?" Uncle Hugo asked incredulously as Esme returned with her supplies.

Esme tried to ignore the stinging remark as she opened the bag and looked through its contents. She checked the amperage on the generator—fifty amps, just like theirs—so she was confident these parts would do the job.

“Lilou,” Jérôme said, “can you go back to the Girouxs’ and see if you can get ahold of an electrician at this hour?”

“I’ll try,” Lilou said. “But I really think in the meantime, you should give Esme a shot at this. She may be able to do it.”

CHAPTER 10

THE LONGEST NIGHT

"This is a far cry from a radio with a six-volt battery," Jérôme said to his wife. "We could have cows dying of pneumonia and infection in there," he gestured toward the barn. "They are *suffering*."

Emotions and tensions were running high. The obstinate pelting of icy rain continued, still assaulting every exposed surface like an oppressive force against which there was no defense.

Esme said a silent prayer, pleading for help to remember all she had learned about electrical circuits and connections.

"Can we move the generator to the panel box of the milking barn?" Esme asked the men, who stood watching her skeptically.

Uncle Hugo looked hesitantly at Jérôme, who shrugged his shoulders wearily, his eyes vacant, and went to one side of the generator, bending his knees and grabbing hold. Uncle Hugo lifted his eyebrows in an expression of unease, let out an uncertain breath, and finally grabbed the other side.

Jérôme and Uncle Hugo lifted the whole machine, carrying it to the milking barn's panel box just outside the barn door. Henri had already removed four screws and lifted off the front cover. Luc and Henri held a tarp up like an awning over the generator and panel box, wide enough for Esme to have a dry workspace. Jérôme held a flashlight to illuminate her work and then handed Esme a pair of thick safety work gloves. "Make sure you put these on," he cautioned.

Esme pulled them onto her hands, wriggling her fingers in the oversized gloves. She set out each item from the wiring kit: a fifty-amp breaker, an eight-gauge wiring cable, a fifty-amp power inlet box, and a metal interlock kit, as well as a screwdriver. The bawling of the cattle was like a ticking time bomb. She felt the pressure not only to relieve their misery, but also to assuage the skepticism of her audience. Luc, Jérôme, Henri, and Uncle Hugo all watched intently.

"Now hold on a second," Jérôme said. "Did we check to be sure all possible voltage to the barn is shut off?"

"Papa," Esme reminded her father gently, "the electrical line is completely snapped, so there is no way for electricity to come in. But yes, there is no chance of electrical shock because I'm wiring the barn to *receive* electricity from the generator."

“Okay,” her father responded. “But I want to be the one to handle the breakers and power, understand?” The concern was thick in his voice.

Esme nodded and then gingerly picked up the thick orange cable and peeled it partway down to reveal the red, black, white, and green coated wires inside. With wire strippers, she cut and exposed half an inch of the copper inside each of the four colored wires.

Following Esme’s directions, Jérôme moved each of the breakers down to free up the top location for installation of the new fifty-amp breaker under the main breaker and to make room for the interlock kit.

Esme’s mind felt clear. She could picture exactly where each wire needed to go based on the images she had studied earlier that day. *Wow, it seems like three days ago*, she thought. Moving with a dexterity surprising even to herself, she threaded the wires into their proper places, securing them tightly with the screwdriver.

“How is it coming?” Lilou asked, walking with her flashlight to the immersed group hovering around the panel box.

“I just need to do one last thing, and then we’ll see,” Esme said. She paused and looked at her mother. “Where are Alice and her sisters?” she asked, suddenly remembering they were in the house and feeling anxious about their well-being.

“They are all asleep on our sectional,” her mother assured her with a smile. “I just went in to check on them and covered each one with a warm blanket. Chantal and Jacques are still cleaning up water in their basement."

"Did you find an electrician?" Jérôme asked.

"Miraculously, I did," Lilou said. "He will be here in about forty minutes." It was nearly eleven fifteen. Every minute on the clock seemed like precious time slipping through their fingers.

Esme had no intention of waiting for the electrician. She screwed the interlock kit into place on the panel box, and then her father plugged in the fifty-amp cord from the generator to the power inlet box she had just wired up. He powered on the generator.

"Okay, Papa, you can try switching the breaker now," she instructed.

Jérôme walked back over to the panel box and said, "Here goes nothing." He double-checked that the interlock kit on the panel was in the correct position to keep the main breaker off. Esme closed her eyes and said a silent prayer. Her heart pounded as she watched her father switch the newly installed breaker to ON.

Nothing happened.

What did I do wrong? Esme thought, feeling her face flush red hot.

Her papa gave her a loving pat on the shoulders. "I'm still impressed, Esme. That was a valiant attempt. 'A' for effort," he said as he turned away, powered off the generator, and headed toward the barn door, Uncle Hugo following. "The electrician should be here soon."

"That would've been crazy if it had worked!" Luc said, ruffling the top of his little sister's hair.

He and Henri laid the tarp over the generator and headed toward the house.

"Is there any food left in there?" Henri asked.

"Hopefully," Luc replied. "There was a lot, but it's gonna be cold now."

"I'll eat anything!" Henri said.

What went wrong? What went wrong? Esme wracked her brain for any kind of insight as to why her wiring didn't work.

"I'm so sorry, sweetie." Maman placed a loving hand on her shoulder.

"Can I borrow that?" Esme asked, snatching the flashlight from her mother's grasp. "And could you switch off the new breaker?" Lilou nodded, confusion evident in her pinched brows.

Esme carefully examined the wiring, double-checking that each wire was secured tightly in place. She bit her lip. "Wait a minute . . ."

Hurrying past her mother into the barn workshop, she shined the light on the shelves, her eyes scanning them for the manual she had returned earlier that day. "There you are!" she cried out, pulling off her safety gloves and snatching it up. She flipped to page nineteen: "Electrical Connections."

She ran her finger over the page, devouring the words like her life depended on it—and perhaps some bovine lives did. "Ah! That's it!" she said as she ran back out to the panel box. Pulling the gloves back on, she made a small adjustment by moving a wire to a different position and securing it in place. Lilou watched her carefully the whole time.

"Okay, Maman. Can you power the generator back up?" It rumbled to life. At the sound of the motor, Luc and Henri popped their heads out the back door to see what was going on. Esme nodded to her mother, who shifted the interlock plate up and switched the breaker on.

The lights popped on in the barn! Henri let out the loudest whoop Esme had ever heard. He and Luc came running, Luc slipping and sliding because he wasn't wearing his ice cleats, Henri holding a bowl of cold dinner. Lilou threw her arms around Esme, laughing and crying at the same time.

Jérôme swung around the edge of the barn door with Uncle Hugo on his heels. "Did the electrician already come?" Jérôme asked.

Esme stood by the panel box, beaming. Lilou was bouncing with joy next to her, her eyes wet with tears.

"Well, now," Uncle Hugo said with an abashed smile on his face. "I do believe I owe you an apology, young lady."

"Apology accepted," Esme smiled as she did a small curtsy and then flung the safety gloves to the side.

"You did it, Esme?" Jérôme questioned as he tromped toward her. "You did it!" He scooped her up in his arms, swung her around, and set her down. "Ha-ha!" he shouted jubilantly. "What are we all waiting for? Let's get to work!"

With renewed energy unusual for the late hour, everyone went to their stations and worked with a vitality and vigor they had never known before. Jérôme asked Esme to be a runner, going between stations to see if anyone needed anything, then fetching what was needed.

Jérôme and Luc worked as swiftly as they could in the milking parlor. Lilou made sure the watering troughs were being filled by the well pump. They were, but the parched cows were drinking the water as quickly as it came in, fighting each other for a turn. Uncle Hugo and Henri hand-fed the cattle with hay because the silo unloader required electricity, and there was only power in the milking barn. They would also need to clean out the stalls, run the gutter cleaner, and then carry buckets of water from the milking barn to the heifer barn, where there was no electricity.

About twenty minutes into their work, Esme noticed lights coming up the drive. It was almost midnight at this point. *That must be the electrician*, she thought. Since everyone else was hard at work, Esme walked out to greet him.

"Hello, I believe an electrician was needed here?" the man said.

"Was" being the operative word, Esme thought. "Yes, but we managed to get things wired up okay," she said.

"Oh, I see," he said, his eyes on the lights of the barn, the generator humming next to it. "Mind if I take a look?" he said, treading carefully.

"Go ahead," Esme said.

The electrician made his way to the panel box and looked it over scrupulously. "Not bad," he said. "Did an electrician do this?" he asked.

"An electrician in training," Esme said, a sparkle in her eye.

"Oh. I see," he said, blinking.

"What about this generator?" Esme motioned toward their broken generator, and they walked to it. "We think it needs a new rotor or stator."

The electrician shined his flashlight and looked it over. "I believe you are right. Unfortunately, those parts have to be sent for." He paused. "Is there an adult I can speak to?"

"I think you spoke to Maman," Esme said. "I'll go get her." Esme found her mother hauling buckets of water from the milk barn to the heifer barn.

Esme overheard them briefly discussing payment for his service call during off-hours.

As the electrician was leaving, another set of lights came up the drive. It was Chantal and Jacques.

"How is the basement?" Esme asked as the couple stepped out of their van.

"We will see," Chantal said. "We've cleaned up the water as best we can tonight."

“How can we help here?” Jacques asked as they got out of their van and headed toward the barn.

“We really need help cleaning out the stalls,” Esme said. She showed them how it was done, and they went to work, Esme included.

When the milking and feeding were done, Jérôme and Luc ran the gutter cleaner and cleared out all the excrement. Luc took loads of manure to their manure pit with the tractor. Uncle Hugo and Henri helped haul water to the other barn, as did Esme and the Girouxs when they finished the stalls.

The work was finally completed at three o’clock in the morning. That’s when everyone realized something: The rain had stopped!

“I’m sorry I have to take the generator,” Uncle Hugo said, “but I’m going to need it tomorrow.”

“We understand,” Jérôme replied, reaching out to shake Uncle Hugo’s hand and then pulling him into a hug. “You’ve bought us another twelve hours to find a generator. How can we ever thank you for coming all this way and staying to help?”

“Just pay it forward.” Uncle Hugo smiled wearily as he switched the generator off.

“Look!” Esme said, her head craned back as she gazed upward. For the first time all week, they could see stars sparkling in the sky.

CHAPTER 11

BLEAK REALITY

It was a relief to have a quiet barn.

After hanging up her soaked coat, Esme lumbered to her bedroom, where she peeled off her wet clothing and quickly pulled on some soft sweats and a hoodie, her teeth chattering all the while. Too tired even to wash up, she made herself a little nest of blankets on the floor next to the sectional where Alice and her sisters had long been asleep—Chantal and Jacques had opted to let their daughters stay while they went home to rest in their own bed.

Esme snuggled down deep into her blankets. A shiver went up her spine as she listened to the howling wind outside. She wondered how they would do their next milking as she drifted off to sleep.

On Saturday morning the sun poured in through the windows for the first time in days. Esme's groggy eyes opened to see Alice and her sisters still bundled up, asleep on the sofa. She noticed she could see her breath inside the house. Her body still heavy with sleep, she got up to use the toilet. Without electricity the well pump didn't run, so they had to keep a bucket full of water next to the toilet and dump it in to flush. While they'd had the generator to power the well pump, Lilou had brought several buckets of water and filled the tub to use for flushing. There was a bowl of water on the counter next to the sink with a small ladle in it for washing: one ladleful to wet each hand and one more to rinse the soap off each hand. It was awkward, and the frigid water made Esme's cold hands even colder.

Upon exiting the restroom, Esme noticed a note written in her mother's handwriting on the family message board magnetized to the fridge:

We've gone to see if the army has a generator. Hoping to be back with one by noon or sooner. —Maman and Papa

P.S. There's cereal for breakfast.

Esme wondered what time her parents had left. They could not have had much sleep—it had probably been a restless night knowing they had no generator and worrying over how the next milking and chores would be accomplished.

Wiping the sleep from her eyes, Esme turned on her radio.

". . . highly encouraged, even urged, to go to a shelter. With temperatures so low, it is not safe to be without a source of heat. Hypothermia is a real threat.

Everyone is so happy the rain has stopped, they forget low temperatures are another beast to wrangle during a power outage this time of year. The power company estimates power will be restored in a week to urban areas, whereas for rural areas it could be another two weeks or more."

Esme's mouth was hanging open in dismay when Luc stumbled in, scratching his belly.

"You're catching flies," he teased, then yawned.

"Yeah, so are you," Esme quipped. "Luc, they're saying power may not be restored for two weeks or more!"

"Seriously?" he asked, incredulous. "We really need a generator. The cattle won't survive without one."

"Yeah, and what about us? They said hypothermia is a real threat. And temperatures are supposed to get a lot colder tonight and tomorrow," Esme said. "Look." She breathed out a frosty *huff* into the air. "You can see my breath!"

"It looks smelly. Go brush," he said.

Esme frowned.

"Hey, you really took charge last night. That was amazing. You keep on reading those electrical manuals, little sis," Luc said, giving Esme a high five.

A rush of warmth—one she planned to hold on to—washed over her, despite the chill in the air.

"Maman?" came a small voice from the couch.

"Reine! Good morning!" Esme chirped enthusiastically, hoping to keep the little girl from another meltdown.

Alice woke up then. "Did you even sleep last night, Esme?"

Just then, there was a knock at the back door.

"It's your parents!" Esme said, observing Jacques and Chantal in the door's large window. She hurried to let them in.

"Long time no see," Jacques said. "Short night, eh?"

"Maman!" Reine cried out. Her mother sat down on the couch and snuggled her.

"Yeah. My parents left before I even woke up." Esme pointed to the whiteboard. "The cows have to be milked about every twelve hours. They don't care if there's a power outage."

"I wish we could do something to help," Chantal said.

"You did!" Luc said. "You came in clutch last night!"

"Well, everyone must be pretty hungry. I know I am!" Jacques rubbed his belly dramatically.

"We have enough cereal for everyone," Esme said, chuckling as she pulled a couple of boxes from the pantry.

"How would everyone like a hot meal?" Jacques asked. "The shelter has pretty good food. Esme and Luc, you can come with us. It will give us all a chance to warm up, too."

"Sounds good to me," Esme agreed, glancing at Luc.

"Well," Luc shrugged, "we can't do anything here without a generator, so . . . why not?" He patted his stomach. "I'll go see if Henri wants to come," Luc said as he dashed up the stairs and then appeared again a moment later. "He says he will stay here in case Maman and Papa get back sooner rather than later and need help."

After leaving a note on the message board and assuring Henri they would bring him some hot food, the group loaded into the Girouxs' van and headed out.

The shelter was at a local junior high. Cots were set up across half the gymnasium as well as in classrooms. The other half of the gym was lined with tables and chairs. The shelter was packed with all sorts of people, young and old: families, single people, even a very pregnant woman with her husband.

"She looks like she is about to have a baby any minute," Esme whispered to Alice, eyeing the woman's enormous belly.

"Yeah, her name is Khanh," Alice whispered back. "She is from Vietnam. I met her in the lunch line a couple of days ago. This is her first baby and her first year in Canada."

"Wow. Welcome to Canada," Esme muttered under her breath. "That seems like it would be kind of scary."

"A lot scary, if you ask me," Alice said, "being in a different country so far from family, about to have a baby with all of this going on. She's really nice, though. So is her husband. They said when the ice storm hit and the power outage happened, they just assumed it was a normal winter in Canada."

Esme noticed how caring Khanh's husband was toward his wife, making sure she was comfortable as she ate her breakfast.

The girls stood in a line and picked up steaming plates of food, then found an empty table in the cafeteria. The French toast with sausage, eggs, milk, and orange juice tasted incredible.

"Who's making all the food?" Esme asked.

"It's all volunteers," Alice replied.

"Wow." Esme was impressed. "They know what they're doing."

"Never thought I would enjoy cafeteria food so much," Luc said with an empty, syrupy plate in his hands and a sticky smile on his face.

A ball rolled over and stopped as it hit Luc's foot. He picked it up and looked around, his eyes landing on an expectant little boy who stood about ten feet away, watching the teen intently. Luc tossed the ball gently to the child, lighting up the little guy's face with an ear-to-ear grin. The boy, who looked to be about two years old, tossed the ball back with surprising accuracy. The game continued back and forth for several minutes until the toddler got distracted and ran off.

Esme noticed a large poster that had been handwritten with a schedule of activities for children, such as a coloring contest, a Hula-Hoop tournament, a mariachi band, and even a comedy show.

"This looks like it could actually be fun!" Esme said.

"Yeah. C'mon," Alice said, taking Esme by the hand. "You have to come meet Cora. When we first came, she was sitting at a table by herself, just staring at nothing. Then one of the volunteers here asked her to help with some of the kids' activities. She's been a lot happier since then."

Alice took Esme to the gymnasium. "There she is!" They walked up to an older woman who was seated at a table, folding and creasing papers with a little girl sitting next to her. The woman had short, permed silver hair and wore a purple muumuu dress. "Cora! This is my friend, Esme."

Cora smiled up at them. "Hello, Alice! Hello, Esme. It's nice to meet you. This is Lauren." She gestured toward the little companion next to her.

"Hi, Cora," Esme greeted her. "What are you doing? Origami? I love origami."

"Sit down! I'll show you two how to make a crane. I just learned myself! It's very entertaining. And while we fold, you can tell me your story. Where are you from?" Cora asked Esme as she handed each girl a square of colored paper.

"I live on a dairy farm outside Gatineau," Esme answered. "How about you?"

"Oh, I live in a condo in town," replied Cora.

"Do you live alone?" Esme asked.

"Yep. Have now for thirty years."

"I bet you miss your home," Esme said.

"Not. One. Bit." Cora emphasized each word. "I mean, I thought I would. But I haven't had this much fun in years—maybe decades!" She laughed so heartily it made Alice and Esme laugh too. Then she quieted and added, "Sometimes the bleakest situation turns out to be the greatest blessing."

The two girls and Cora enjoyed chatting as the controlled chaos buzzed around them.

At ten thirty there was a reptile show. A local pet store had volunteered to entertain the children for forty-five minutes with snakes, lizards, and turtles. Alice was holding a bearded dragon and Esme had a snake when Luc came up and said, "We'd better see if the Girouxs can take us home. Papa and Maman are going to need help. Let's hope they found a generator."

Esme was having so much fun she wished she could stay for the comedy show at three o'clock, but she knew that Luc was right. They stopped at the cafeteria for a bag of food for Henri on their way out.

CHAPTER 12

BLESSINGS AND LOSS

When they pulled up the drive, the pickup truck was there, but Esme noticed there was no generator under the awning nor at the panel box she had wired up the night before. The realization felt heavy. Luc's shoulders slumped. He had noticed, too.

"We will bring some dinner tonight, okay?" Chantal promised as Luc and Esme slid out of the van.

"See you soon!" Alice said cheerfully.

But the cheer Esme had felt moments before had evaporated. She and Luc hurried into the house. Their parents were seated at the dinner table, Jérôme's head in his hands and Lilou's eyes and nose red, a pile of used tissues next to her.

They both stood abruptly to greet their children.

"The army didn't have any generators?" Luc ventured, seemingly alarmed to see his parents in this state of distress.

Lilou shook her head as she gave Luc a hug and kissed Esme on the top of her head.

"Maybe we should say a prayer," Esme offered innocently.

"Absolutely, we should," Jérôme agreed.

They all knelt together in the family room and joined hands.

"Since it was your idea, would you like to say the prayer for us, Esme?" her papa asked.

As Esme began, she took a moment to consider ways in which God had already blessed and taken care of them.

"Dear God, You have helped us all through this storm so far. You have helped us take care of the cows. We have had enough food. Uncle Hugo brought his generator, and You helped me have the knowledge I needed to wire it up last night. You have blessed us with kind neighbors who came and helped us. And the rain finally stopped. Thank You, God. We are really thankful for these things."

Esme was no stranger to turning to God when she needed help with something. Knowing He answered prayers, she had no problem asking Him for help. "You know, God, that we can't take care of our farm without a generator—a big one. Maman and Papa have tried so hard to find one. They've done everything they can think of. They were prepared with one when the storm hit. They were so kind to share it with neighbors who were in need, even though it made life harder for us, but they wanted to help; then it broke. You helped us find Uncle Hugo, but that generator couldn't stay. They have tried to buy a new one, but there are none to be found. Maman called the radio station. We have gone to the military for help, but they don't have generators, either. Dear God, we don't know what else to do. But we know You care about us and You care about our cows. We are all Yours. So please, God. Please help us find a generator."

As Esme closed the prayer, her mother sniffed and wiped her eyes. Luc squeezed his sister's hand in appreciation. Jérôme kept his head bowed, then finally lifted it. Blinking hard, he cleared his throat. "Thank you, sweetheart." He paused as he stood and moved back to the dinner table. The family followed him, sitting down together.

"Where's Henri?" Luc asked.

"Since roads are better and there is nothing to do here now, he went to check on things at his place," Lilou said. "He plans to be back around milking time, but . . ." she trailed off.

Jérôme cleared his throat again. "We know God helps in His way and His timing, not always in the way we want or hope for. I think we need to prepare ourselves for the possibility that we could lose some cows. Henri and I were with them an hour ago. We treated four of them for mastitis, and several others are showing signs of pneumonia." He spoke with solemn resignation, his eyes focused on a spot on the table. His hair was disheveled, the sides and back molded by the leather band of his cowboy hat. Each time the generator had been on, powering the well pump and water heater, he had been working to take care of the cows, so he hadn't been able to shower for nearly a week.

Esme looked at the clock—eleven ten. Milking should ideally be started again in an hour or two. Esme gazed out the kitchen window and noticed the eaves draped in icicles that sparkled in the morning sun. She suddenly felt an urgent desire to go out and be alone in nature. "I'm going outside," she said.

Lilou looked at Esme questioningly. "What for?"

Esme shrugged. "I just want to."

"Okay. Be sure to wear your ice cleats. It's still slick out there," her mother warned. "And stay away from the eaves of the house and barn; chunks of ice have been sliding off."

Esme slipped her wool-socked feet into her cleated boots and pulled on her mittens. As she was walking out the back door, Lilou called, "Oh, and stay away from trees! Branches are still breaking!"

"Okay, Maman," Esme said a little impatiently, closing the door abruptly behind her, happy for some time alone.

In the sunlight the world around her glistened like uniquely crafted crystal sculptures. The snow that had fallen before the ice storm was now crusted with ice.

She walked beyond the barns to the edge of the dormant alfalfa field and squinted across the clearing that stretched out for acres, covered in a pristine, wintry-white blanket. She remembered a time when her father had taken her for a ride across that field on a sled tied to the tractor with a long rope.

She took a step onto the snowy blanket. Her foot lingered on top for a brief moment before crunching in a few inches, creating a stiff-edged footprint. She took another step, then another, and another, finding immense satisfaction with each delightful crunch. It reminded her of the sugary crust on a perfectly torched crème brûlée. Turning to see the pattern of prints created in the crisp snow, Esme felt a sense of artistry, as if the field were a canvas and she had just started her own unique design.

Walking methodically, she created a curve in the pattern here and there, which made an interesting line of footprints to look back on. Standing in the middle of the field, she looked all around her and noticed how unusually still and quiet everything seemed. No farm equipment could be heard, no cars on the road below their property, no motors at all. Not even the sound of birds was present. She lay down, spreading out her arms and legs, grateful for her hooded thigh-length coat to keep out the cold.

Closing her eyes, Esme enjoyed the sun on her face, glad for a little time free of worry, time to simply *be*.

Her favorite Bible verse came to mind: *Be still, and know that I am God.* She expressed gratitude to God for the quiet, peaceful moment she was enjoying. She felt an unusual warmth settle over her, despite lying flat in the icy field. It was a feeling of peace, like everything would be okay. She lay for a long time, savoring the stillness, peace, and assurance.

A motor broke the silence. As it drew near, she listened closely, trying to determine where it was headed. It would likely keep going until the sound faded into the distance. But it didn't fade. It got louder, which meant one thing: It had pulled onto their property.

Esme bolted upright. She could see a vehicle coming up their drive. Was it a pickup truck? It kind of looked like Brewster's blue truck. He must be hoping that her parents had located a generator he could borrow; he was most certainly in the same dire straits they were. As his engine turned off, Esme plopped back down in the snow, her coat providing a pleasant insulation. She closed her eyes again, sorry for his imminent disappointment. As expected, his vehicle started up again. She listened as the motor grew faint and disappeared into the distance.

After a few minutes, she heard another motor. The sound was not fading. *Wait a minute. That doesn't sound like Brewster's truck, or any other vehicle for that matter. That sounds like . . .*

Esme jumped up. She started for the house, running

haphazardly across the field as fast as she could, tripping multiple times on the icy edges of her footprints, which grabbed onto her bulky snow boots. *Could it be? Could it really be?* she thought as she raced closer, the roar of the motor growing louder. She didn't dare believe it until she saw . . .

"A generator!" she yelped. A big one! And it was hooked up to their pole switch, roaring away like it meant business! "Where is everyone?" Esme yelled, her excitement bubbling over. She ran into the house and heard the bathtub running. "Maman?" she called out.

The bathroom door was wide open, but no one was in there. She was grateful she came in when she did because one more minute and the tub would have overflowed. She turned the faucet knob until the flow stopped. *What is going on? Where is my family?*

She headed toward the back door. *I'll go check the barn*, she thought. But before she went out, she stopped at the grouping of light switches by the door and flipped the kitchen light on and off, on and off, satisfaction spreading across her face in a joyful smile as she relished the miracle of light bulbs. She could hear the furnace running and the fan blowing warm air out through the vents. The refrigerator motor was also humming.

They must be choring, she thought as she ran toward the milk barn. Before she reached the barn door, however, she saw her papa, who was running the silo unloader into the feed mixer on the tractor. As soon as he caught sight of Esme, he stopped what he was doing and switched off the unloader. He hopped down from the tractor and strode toward his daughter in sure, unwavering steps. Pulling her into a tight hug, he held on for several seconds before kissing the top of her head and taking a step back, his hands on her shoulders.

"You must have a direct line to Heaven, Esme," he said, his eyes soft, emitting an inner glow.

"Where did the generator come from?" Esme asked.

"Brewster. He was able to buy one."

Surprised, she asked, "But how? You've tried everything to get one."

"Apparently, he showed up at just the right time, when the dealer was unloading a new shipment," Jérôme explained. "He did his milking and then brought it over. He intends to share with us now until the power is back up."

Esme considered this turn of events for a moment. "That wasn't just an answer to my prayers, Papa. You did the first kind deed by sharing with Brewster and Mr. Fotakis. I thought you were kind of crazy to do that. But it really is true what they say, eh?"

"What's that?" Jérôme leaned in, ear first, his cowboy hat tipping to the side.

"What goes around comes around," Esme quipped.

"I think someone else said it even better: 'Whatsoever ye would that men should do to you, do ye even so to them.'"

"Oh yeah!" Esme said as she recalled the Bible verse. "He knew what He was talking about, didn't He?"

"I believe we can trust that He did. And does," Jérôme said, patting a loose fist against his chest, pointing up, then pointing at Esme affectionately, a warm smile on his face.

As soon as they finished chores, every family member took a turn with a quick shower before returning the generator to Brewster.

"Why was the tub downstairs running full blast while everyone was choring today?" Esme called out to Lilou while towel-drying her wet hair.

"Oh, I forgot to turn it off! Did you do it?" Her mother's face looked panic-stricken.

"Yeah. When I came in, it was about to overflow," Esme said.

"Oh, bless you, child!" Lilou exclaimed. "I turned it on when it got really cold in the house to try to drain the pipes—I was worried the water would freeze and crack them. I guess I forgot to turn it off!"

"Well, I put the stopper in, so now we have plenty of water to flush with while we are without power."

When the Girouxs arrived a couple of hours later, as promised, Esme ran outside to greet them. Alice was the first one out of the van.

"Esme! Do I have a story for you!"

CHAPTER 13

MIRACLES

The other three Giroux girls spilled out of the van after Alice. Immediately, they were all talking at Esme with a fervor unequal to any interaction she had ever had with them. It was such a clamor that she only caught a few words: "Khanh," "funny," and "ambulance."

"Wait! Hold on." Chantal got the four girls' attention. "I know you are all excited, but Esme can't listen to all of you at once. Be quiet and let Alice talk," she said definitively.

Alice was so excited she hardly seemed to notice her little sisters' interference but continued on with her story. "We were all watching the comedy show this afternoon at the shelter. The comedian was in the middle of a joke when a bunch of firefighters whooshed into the back of the gym. They put someone on a stretcher, then left. There were so many of them, we couldn't really see the stretcher, but one of the volunteers told me that it was Khanh and that she was going to the hospital to have her baby!"

"Yeah, and we might get to see her baby later!" Inés said.

"The comedian even had to start over on his joke because he got distracted and forgot what he was saying!" Gisèle said, stifling a giggle with a hand over her mouth.

Jacques and Chantal were both carrying paper bags full of food. "Shall we go in and eat?" Jacques asked.

As they walked into the house, Esme said, "Do you want to hear about a miracle that happened today?"

"Yes! What was it?" Alice replied.

"A generator appeared as an answer to my family's prayers!" Esme said.

"Really?" Alice replied.

"Yes! Well, it didn't just appear; our neighbor brought one over, and he will share it with us until the power is back," Esme explained.

Lilou was lighting new candles on plates around the kitchen and on the dining table. "The food smells delicious! Thank you for bringing it! Won't you all stay and eat it with us?"

"Only if it's by candlelight," Chantal jested.

"Well, you won't believe what I have planned! Dinner by candlelight!" Lilou laughed.

After Alice blessed the food, everyone dished up paper plates of ravioli, breadsticks, and Caesar salad.

"Have you had a chance to scope out the damage to your sugar bush yet?" Jérôme asked Jacques, pausing before eating a forkful of ravioli, which was quickly followed by a breadstick.

Jacques swallowed a bite of salad and let out a long exhale. "It's hard to tell how bad it is just yet. We won't know until we can go in there. Until the ice melts, it's too dangerous. I don't know, Jérôme. It's not looking good."

"I'm sorry, my friend," Jérôme said. "What can we do to help?"

"You know, honestly, we are going to need a lot of help cleaning up downed branches. It'll be a huge project. I'm concerned about getting that done in time to tap what trees have survived. Plus, repairs need to be made to the sugar shack, and now there is water damage in the basement. It all seems really overwhelming." His shoulders were slumped.

Esme suddenly had an idea. "What if we organize a sugar bush cleanup?" Her grin at Alice was like passing a baton.

"Yeah," Alice said, taking the baton and running with it, "and we could make a bunch of posters and put them up. We could put some in the shelter and any place that has a bulletin board."

"I bet we could put an ad in the newspaper," Lilou said.

"And we could call it 'Save the Sugar Shack,'" said Alice.

"How about 'Sugar Bush Service Bash'?" Esme offered.

"I like both names!" Jacques said, brightening.

"Yeah, and we could make it fun and have maple treats," added Gisèle.

Alice lit up. "Esme and I could offer free babysitting while parents come help!"

"It would be great practice for our adventure camp later this summer!" Esme was getting excited.

"I'll help if I can use a chain saw!" Luc inserted.

"Oh, we will need plenty of chain saws," Jacques said, his demeanor elevated significantly compared to the previous few minutes.

The families settled on January 31 as the Save the Sugar Shack/Sugar Bush Service Bash date. After dinner Esme brought out paper and crayons. All the girls wanted to help make posters.

"Want to help, Luc?" Esme offered him a sheet of paper.

"Nah. But when the chain saws come out, count me in!" he said.

All five girls joyfully crafted their posters by candlelight as the adults chatted, laughing often. Despite the still-frigid air inside the house, the atmosphere was filled with a warmth that could only come from friends supporting each other. After the stress of the week, the evening proved to be a balm for everyone's spirits.

As the Giroux family was leaving, everyone exchanged warm hugs.

"Are you sure you will all be okay here tonight?" Chantal asked. "It's really cold out there. The forecast is saying it will be even colder tomorrow—the coldest day of the season so far."

"Brewster should be back with the generator any time now, and we can keep it all night, so we will have heat," Jérôme said.

"Yeah, I'm going to make a bed right on top of the vent!" Esme said with joyful anticipation. Everyone had remained bundled in their coats all evening due to the chill in the house.

Alice's family took the stack of colorful, diversely designed posters to distribute. "It will give us something to do," Chantal said.

After the Girouxs left, Esme turned to her family. "That was really fun. I feel so happy."

"I agree," replied Lilou. "Did you notice how they all left with smiles too? Even Jacques."

"Yeah, it's a huge blessing having such great friends and neighbors, isn't it?" Jérôme added.

"I think it's quite miraculous," said Esme, smiling.

❄ ❄ ❄

Three days later, on the ninth day without power, another miracle happened. They had just finished morning chores and returned the generator to Brewster. Esme was enjoying her hour of school reading time when she noticed an unfamiliar mint-green pickup truck coming up their drive.

"Someone is here!" Esme called out.

"Who is it?" Lilou called back from the laundry room.

"I don't know. Some guy— Oh, looks like Luc is going to talk to him. Papa is walking over too," Esme said, and she went back to her book.

Several minutes later, Luc burst in through the back door. "You are not going to believe this!" he exclaimed.

Lilou came running down the hall. "What? Who was that?" She moved around Luc to look out the back window. The truck had left.

"The guy gets out and says, 'Is this the Errard residence?' I'm like, 'Yeah, man, what's it to ya?'"

Lilou gasped. "You did not say that!"

"Nah, just kidding." He grinned. "I said, 'Yes, how can I help you?'"

Lilou exhaled a sigh of relief. She had gone to great lengths to teach her children proper manners.

Luc continued, "The guy says, 'I have a delivery here for you.' Papa walks up, and we follow the delivery guy to his truck bed. It's a fifty-kilowatt generator!"

"What?" Lilou said as she put on her boots and coat, shock and disbelief spread across her face. "But who's it from?"

"He said it was from an anonymous donor. Something about the radio station?"

"CFRA?" Esme shouted. By this time she was also putting on boots and a coat to go outside.

"That sounds right," Luc said as the three of them hurried out the door and ran to the pole switch, where Jérôme was unpackaging the large generator.

"Is this ours?" Lilou cried when she reached her husband. "Is it really ours?"

Jérôme already had wet eyes and cheeks. Lilou fell into his arms and sobbed tears of relief and gratitude.

"The man who brought it said a call was made to CFRA and someone had this sent over."

"But who?" Lilou blubbered.

"He wouldn't say. I don't think he knew. He was just the delivery guy," Jérôme said with a quiver in his voice.

"Do we get to have the generator all the time?" Esme asked.

"Looks like it," Jérôme said with a tearful chuckle. "Brewster has one, and he said Mr. Fotakis has one now too." He ran a sleeve across his nose, his bottom lip trembling.

Esme didn't think things could get any better, but a couple of hours later, Jacques came over with Alice. They invited her to go back with them to the shelter for a few hours. "You get to come to comedy hour with a clown who makes animals and swords and stuff out of balloons! We got to see him on our first day in the shelter, and he's coming back!"

Before comedy hour started, they made beaded

bracelets with Cora. Esme was impressed by Cora's patience as a teacher. She was gifted at explaining things in a way the children could understand. Even the three- and four-year-olds like Reine had their eyes and attention fixed on her.

"I have an idea," Esme whispered to Alice. "What if we invite Cora to come help with our sugar bush service activity? The kids love her. She could help entertain them with crafts."

Alice's whole face lit up. "Esme, you are brilliant! And I think Cora would love it! It would help her not be all alone in her apartment—if we ever get power back."

"Let's ask her after this class," Esme said. Alice nodded heartily.

Cora was delighted with the invitation. She wrote her phone number down on a piece of paper for the girls. "You have made my whole day! My whole week! My whole month!" Cora cackled joyfully.

During comedy hour, the clown made a pirate hat for Alice and a sword for Esme. "Arr, me hearty!" Esme played, pointing her "sword" at Alice, who giggled and shouted, "Shiver me timbers!" in her best pirate voice.

Then Alice's face grew serious. "There's one more thing we need to do before we take you home."

Esme studied her friend's face, curious.

"We need to go see Khanh!" Alice grinned. "She and her husband came back to the shelter yesterday with their new baby. The volunteers put them in a small classroom so they would have some privacy. Let's go ask if we can visit them!"

"She's here? With the new baby?" Esme squeaked. It had been so long since she had seen a newborn baby.

The volunteer in charge of the classrooms asked Alice and Esme to first wash their hands very well *with soap*, she emphasized. Then she walked the two girls to Room 122. She knocked gently on the door. Khanh's husband answered and invited them in with a slight bow of his head.

Khanh was lying on her side on a cot, a tiny bundle snuggled up against her. Alice and Esme walked in with the awe and reverence the scene demanded. Khanh smiled at the girls and beckoned them nearer with a wave of her hand. They knelt down on the floor in front of Khanh and her baby with wonder.

"Is it a boy or a girl?" Alice asked, peering down at the tiny bundle.

"Boy," Khanh whispered. "His name is Chien. It means *warrior*."

"He's so tiny," Alice said.

Esme watched the swaddled baby with his mass of black hair sleeping peacefully. "He's a miracle," she said.

CHAPTER 14

THAW AND RENEWAL

Esme's walkie-talkie spat out dashes and dots. "Meet in the tunnel?" the code said.

Alice! For all the adventure of the last two weeks, Esme had really missed walkie-talkie Morse code with her best friend.

"Yes!" Esme coded. She left a note on the whiteboard: *Tunnel —E.* She grabbed her clipboard, paper, pen, and a flashlight before dashing out the back door.

In the tunnel, though, Esme was not met with the cheerful demeanor she had come to expect from Alice.

"What's wrong, Alice?" Esme asked.

"The tree house took a lot of damage along with the trees," Alice said, her eyes downcast.

"Oh no," Esme said, putting her hand on Alice's arm.

"A huge branch broke off and fell on it, smashing everything down to the picnic table. It will have to be completely rebuilt."

Esme felt a sudden ache at the loss, as the tree house was a favorite place for the pair during the summers. A lump rose in her throat, and she didn't know what to say.

"And the maple farm is . . ." Alice trailed off. Esme could see a tear glistening, even in the dimness of the flashlights. "Papa and Maman say what's left of it is probably not going to be enough to support our family."

Esme listened quietly, afraid to hear any more, but needing to know what Alice would say next.

"I don't know if we can stay." Alice was barely audible. "Papa is looking for work in the city."

Esme gasped. With her exhale, the lump in her throat escaped in a sob.

Feeling powerless to do anything to change the situation, the friends cried together for a long time. Esme could not imagine anyone else living on the other end of the tunnel. This was her and Alice's tunnel. The Girouxs were like family, the storm having strengthened their bond. The thought of no Morse codes coming through the walkie-talkie ever again was a devastating prospect. She did not want to think about it.

Wiping her tears, Esme said, "We still have the sugar bush cleanup. Let's focus on that. My mother is placing the ad with the newspaper right now."

"We took our posters to all the nearby shelters and grocery stores and even stapled some to telephone posts," Alice sniffed, raking her sleeve across her nose.

"Oh, I hope and pray for a good turnout," Esme said.

"Thank you, Esme," Alice said with shimmering eyes.

"For what?"

"For caring so much about my family and our sugar bush," Alice answered.

"You would do the same for me. Besides, don't thank me until people actually show up for the cleanup," Esme responded, pulling out her clipboard.

"That's not the point," Alice said sincerely. "I mean, no matter what happens with the sugar bush, I will always remember how loved and important you have made me feel."

The friends spent the next hour making plans for the "kids korner" they planned to co-direct with Cora as a helper. They decided Esme would call Cora and make arrangements to have her picked up and brought to the sugar bush on the appointed day. Amidst all the devastation and all the potential bad news, the girls found that working on future plans was far better for their souls than dwelling on the negative. It felt good to focus on what they could do rather than on what they had no power to change.

❄ ❄ ❄

On January 31 the Giroux and Errard families were astonished at the number of people who came to help with the cleanup. Forty-nine adults showed up with gloves, handsaws, and chain saws.

While the adults and Luc worked, Alice, Esme, and Cora entertained fifteen children, including Alice's three little sisters, in the Giroux home. Among other activities, Cora taught them all how to make paper cranes, assisted by Alice and Esme.

The damage to the bush was devastating. At first the mood was somber as everyone worked together. But, as crushing as it was to see the impaired maple trees, spirits were buoyed because of all the caring hands that came out to show love and support.

❄ ❄ ❄

The Girouxs filed an insurance claim that paid for repairs on the sugar shack as well as their basement. By mid-March they were ready to tap the trees. Some of the sugar maples that seemed mortally wounded showed everyone that they were fighters and that they, like so many Canadians, had survived the ice storm. However, as expected, the sap collection was far lower than in previous years. Usually, maple season was a busy, festive time at the sugar shack, but this year's inventory was not enough to support the usual live band, maple treats, and people needed to run the sugar shack.

One April afternoon, Esme and Alice listened to music and continued their plans for their summer adventure camp, even though they were unsure if Alice would still live there in the summer. Esme's mind was unexpectedly sparked with an idea from an advertisement on the radio.

"What if your whole family got involved in the camp?" she proposed.

"What do you mean?" Alice asked.

"We could build obstacle courses and offer camps that build trust and unity for youth groups and even for companies to strengthen relationships among employees. I've heard of that sort of thing! You have this entire hundred acres that is good for more than syrup!"

"Then maybe we could stay!" Alice said, catching Esme's vision. "Let's go tell my parents!" Bubbling with the joy of new possibilities, they ran to find Chantal and Jacques.

"Papa! Maman!" Alice exclaimed as the girls ran into the house from the maple bush. Chantal and Jacques were at the table, bent over stacks of bills, their faces long. "Esme just had the best idea! Tell them, Esme!"

As Esme relayed her idea for a new business venture in the Giroux forest, a glimmer appeared in Jacques's eye.

"We do still have some maple trees producing sap, but not enough," he said, looking toward Chantal. "It is rather smart to consider how else we can use the land without leaving it. We'd still need a loan to cover the initial costs, but I could talk to my friend at the bank to see if it would be possible." Jacques's energy was growing by the second. Chantal's expression began to brighten. "Esme, this is a brilliant idea!" Jacques declared.

The ideas started flowing quickly after that. "We could build a huge ropes course in the middle of the forest," Jacques suggested.

"The sugar shack could be the new headquarters for the camp, like a small convention center," Chantal said. "We could create a trust walk through the forest to the ropes course where people partner up; one partner is blindfolded, being guided and directed over logs and around obstacles by the other partner."

"And they could use walkie-talkies for the trust walk!" Alice added jubilantly.

"And I think campers would love to see the process of tapping trees and boiling the sap to make syrup. Maybe some lessons could be learned with it, like persistence and patience," Esme said.

"The sweetest things in life," quipped Chantal, thinking, "require persistence, patience . . ." she tapped her temple, ". . . and sacrifice!" She grinned at Jacques, who nodded heartily and slapped the table in approval.

Alice and Esme giggled.

"These are great ideas. And I just thought of one: I could partner with the company that does river excursions on the Gatineau River. It could increase business for them and be another attraction to ours!" Jacques spoke like the adventure camp already existed. "Alice, bring me the phone, please!" he requested, a light burning in his eyes.

As she handed her father the phone, Alice bit her

bottom lip to contain her excitement, but she couldn't stop the grin that was spreading across her face. Her eyes shone brightly toward Esme.

A happy tear slipped down Esme's cheek as she said a silent prayer of gratitude that her best friend might be able to remain on the other end of the tunnel after all—that Morse code would continue indefinitely.

The following morning, Esme listened to the talk radio station as she brushed her teeth and got ready for the day.

"Welcome to CFRA this sunny spring morning, April sixteenth." The personality coming through Esme's radio was bright and cheerful. "Happy Thursday, everyone! It has been three months since the ice storm knocked out power for four million Canadians, displacing thousands of people to shelters throughout Quebec. Crews worked sixteen-hour days in below-freezing temps to bring power back to your cities. We are still talking about this, friends. It was a traumatic experience for most people in one way or another!

"It's the top of the nine o'clock hour, and this is the segment where we take your calls and hear your stories. There's something about telling your story that can be healing. If you've had a harrowing experience as a result of the storm, call and tell us about it. If your need was met because you called in, call us back and tell us about it. It can be funny, sad, maddening—it doesn't matter. We want to hear your story."

Should I call in? Esme thought. The idea caused her heart to nearly thump out of her chest. Before she could talk herself out of it, she picked up the phone.

"The lines are now open. Call us at 1-800-580-CFRA. Again, that's . . ."

Esme began to dial, her hands shaking with nervous excitement. She would try just a few times and then—

"Hello! This is 580 CFRA. You're on the air. What is your name?"

Esme was stunned for a moment; she really didn't think she would get through.

"Hello? This is CFRA. Are you there?"

"Hello. Uh, yes," Esme said, suddenly feeling shy and self-conscious. Talking on the radio live was completely unnerving. Why in the world had she decided to call in? Plus, she was hearing herself over the radio with a slight delay, so she quickly turned the volume off.

"What's your name?" the happy voice asked.

"Uh, Esme."

"Hello, Esme. Do you mind me asking how old you are?"

"I'm eleven," Esme said.

"Well, welcome to the show, Esme. Did you have an experience you would like to share?"

"Yes, I do," she began timidly. "I live on a dairy farm. We have 160 head of cattle. Eighty of them have to be milked twice a day."

"My goodness. How did you get through that?"

"It was really hard. Sometimes we didn't know how we would do our next milking. Twice we had to dump all the milk from the cooling tank, which was worth hundreds of dollars . . ."

"Literally down the drain! I've heard this outage has been especially challenging for dairy farmers. A lot of them have not only lost milk down the drain, but they've lost cattle to the storm. Esme, what other losses has your farm suffered?"

"Well, four of our cows got mastitis, and Papa says their milk production will always be lower, but they are okay. We had five with pneumonia, but they got better."

"So, when was power restored to your farm, Esme?"

"On day fourteen."

"So you went two whole weeks without power. You must have had a generator then?"

"We did, but that is one of the reasons I wanted to call. On a night that we were praying for a generator, I heard your radio show, and my mom called in. She didn't make it on air, but a few days later, a brand-new generator was delivered by someone connected to the radio station, and I just want to say thank you." Esme's voice cracked on the last three words.

"Oh, my dear Esme, you are welcome! We love to hear stories like this!"

"But that's not all."

"Okay, go ahead. What else would you like to say?"

Esme grew a little more confident. "Being given a very expensive generator was amazing, more than we ever expected. We all cried. But that wasn't the best thing," Esme said.

"Now you have me really intrigued, Esme. What was the best thing?"

"The best thing was the people who helped. It was our neighbors who came and helped us around midnight when we were so, so tired. They brought us food, too. And we took food to them when they were having a hard time. We helped them when their basement flooded, and they helped us clean the stables so more cows wouldn't get pneumonia.

"It was another neighbor who literally came as an answer to prayer with a generator when we didn't know how we would milk the cows next. We were sharing ours with him before it broke. I realized it was better to share with neighbors and be uncomfortable on the outside because it made me feel so good on the inside."

"Wow." The radio host cleared his throat a couple of times as Esme continued.

"Our neighbors are maple farmers, and they lost most of their trees. But so many friends, neighbors, and even strangers came to help clean up the damage in their sugar bush."

"This is the kind of thing that makes me proud to be a Canadian, folks. Watching people pull together like Esme and her neighbors has been awe-inspiring."

"Do you want to know the other best thing?" Esme asked.

"Absolutely, dear. Tell me. You have all of Quebec on the edge of our seats."

"Well, I learned a lot about myself," Esme said. "I used to feel bad that I'm so small and useless on a farm like ours. My big brother can drive the tractors and do all the heavy lifting that I can't, and some things I've been too afraid to try."

"Uh-huh," the host said. "Keep going."

"Well, I learned that I'm valuable just because I'm me, not for what I can do. And I also learned that there are a lot of things I *can* do to help in my own special way, and that when I use what I can do to help people, I feel really good inside. That's the best thing."

The radio host sniffed, cleared his throat, and said, "Esme, thank you for calling in today, dear."

"Thank you," Esme said.

"You take care now, okay? Bye-bye."

Esme hung up the phone and turned the volume back up on her radio. "Well, there you have it, folks. The best thing. It's not what we have, but what we share. Life lessons from eleven-year-old Esme."

Dots and dashes beeped on the walkie-talkie.

"Coming!" Esme replied as she switched off the radio, grabbed her jacket and flashlight, and zipped out the back door to meet Alice in their tunnel.

PRONUNCIATION & DEFINITION GUIDE

Esme: (EHS–may)

Lilou: (LEE–loo)

Jérôme: (ZHAY–rohm)

Luc: (LEWK)

Errard: (ay–RAWR)

Maman: (MAH–moh); mom/mama

Tu l'as fait: (too lah fay); you did it

Giroux: (zhee–ROO)

Henri: (awn–REE)

Pierre: (pee–AIR)

Jacques: (ZHAWK)

Chantal: (SHAWN–tahl)

Gisèle: (ZHEE–zehl)

Inés: (EE–nes)

Reine: (REN)

Khanh (Vietnamese): (KAWN)

Chien (Vietnamese): (CHEE–en); warrior

Try another Level 5 book from The Good and the Beautiful.

Violet and the Volcanoes: The Mysterious Manor

By Amy Drorbaugh

goodandbeautiful.com

1.0NSP516-163051 Printed in USA Oct-2025